REVISING & EDI 4TH GRADE

By: Carlin Liborio

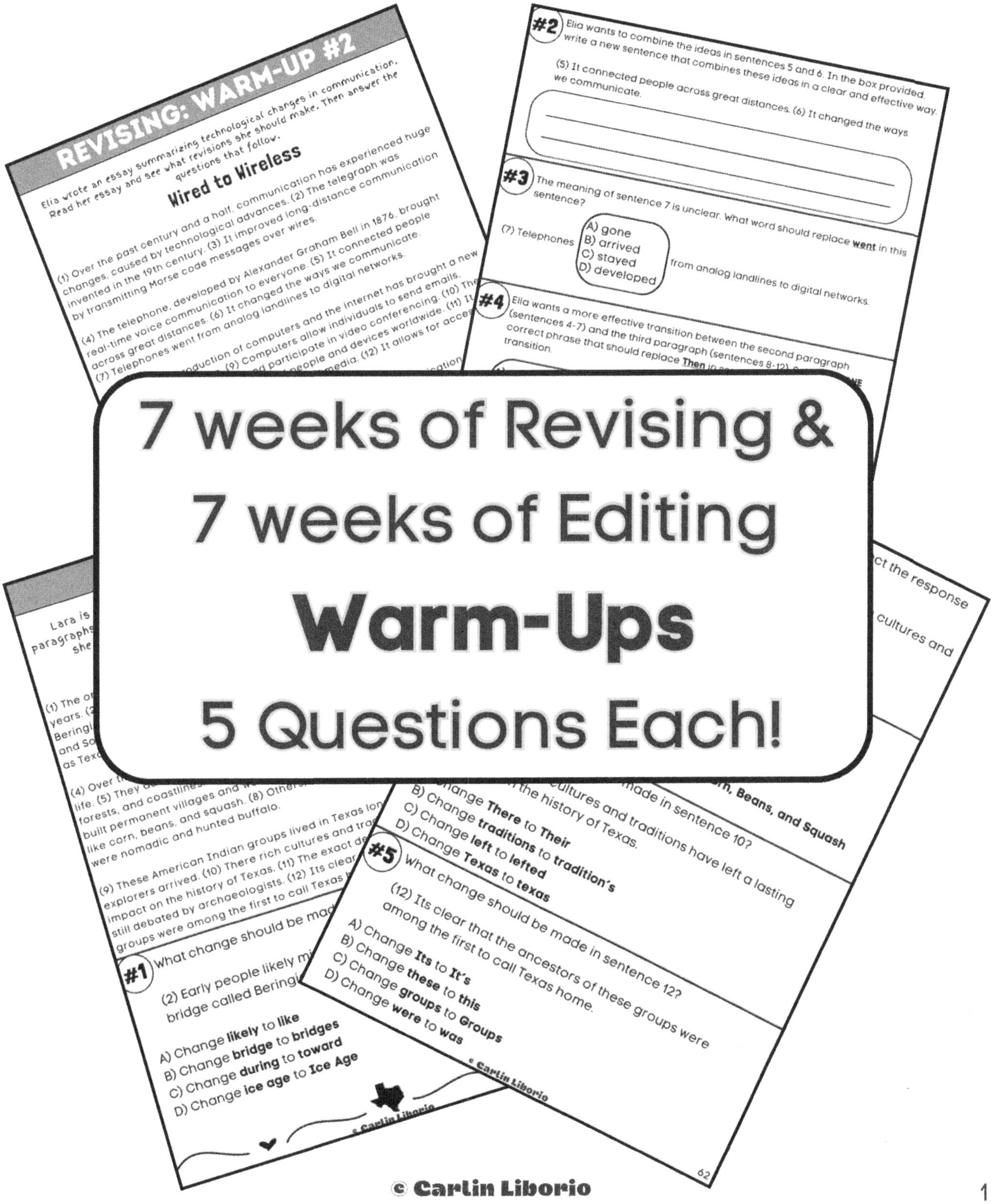

7 weeks of Revising & 7 weeks of Editing Warm-Ups

5 Questions Each!

© Carlin Liborio

Cross-Curricular Social Studies & Science Passages!

7 weeks of Revising & 7 weeks of Editing Practice Pages — 10 Questions Each!

Revising & Editing Student Workbook - 4th Grade:
English Language Arts - 14 Weeks of Daily Warm-Ups + Practice

Copyright ©Carlin Liborio, Liborio Consulting, LLC, 2025-Present.
All rights reserved.

The purchase of this publication entitles the buyer to reproduce pages in this book for single classroom use ONLY. No other part of this publication may be reproduced in whole or in part, or stored in a retrieval system, or distributed or transmitted in any form or by any means. This includes electronic, photocopying, recording, or other electronic or mechanical methods without prior permission of the publisher. No part of this product maybe used or reproduced for commercial use. Contact the author: Carlin@CarlinLiborio.com

ISBN 979-8-9985258-7-2

Join my email list for FREEBIES and tips!
Reading & Writing FREEBIES, important information, and more!
https://carlinliborio.myflodesk.com

Looking for more resources and support?
Follow my teacher Facebook page, subscribe to my YouTube Channel, and sign up for online courses!
https://CarlinLiborio.com

Interested in a purchase order?
Email me for a quote for your campus or district! Discounts on class sets!
Carlin@CarlinLiborio.com

About this Workbook

- This student workbook contains **daily revising and editing warm-up and practice pages** for **fourth-grade** students.

- The passages are **cross-curricular** and integrated with **social studies and science TEKS** (Texas Essential Knowledge and Skills) for **4th grade**.

- The **passages** include **warm-up and practice pages** along with **answer keys**. You may want to remove the answer keys before giving this workbook to students.

- Students can **write directly on the pages** and keep all their warm-ups and practice pages **neatly organized** in **one book**.

- Each student can **practice revising and editing skills directly in their own book**.

- Students can also use their workbook to look back at **previous questions as a review of what they have learned throughout the year.**

Workbook Contents:

Part 1: REVISING

7 Weeks of Warm-Up & Practice STUDENT PAGES

Each week contains:
- A revising **Warm-Up Passage with five questions**
- A revising **Practice Passage with ten questions**

Part 2: EDITING

7 Weeks of Warm-Up & Practice STUDENT PAGES

Each week contains:
- An Editing **Warm-Up Passage with five questions**
- Two Editing **Practice Passages with five questions each (ten questions total)**

Arms/Cups Strategy Cards

Answer Keys for Revising & Editing Warm-Ups and Practice Questions can be found at the back of the book.

**Note: You may remove the answer keys at the back of the book or keep them for students to self-check.

© **Carlin Liborio**

About this Workbook

Why should you use cross-curricular passages integrated with social studies and science?

- This gives students **background knowledge** to help them with **reading comprehension**.

- By integrating **social studies and/or science** with reading and writing, students will **develop high-level academic vocabulary**.

- Students will **make connections across subjects** and recognize the **importance of writing in all subject areas.**

- **Connecting ideas across disciplines** helps students construct knowledge more actively, leading to a **better understanding and retention** of the material.

- Students also benefit from these **time-saving learning opportunities** by seeing how **different subjects are connected**, which provides a **new perspective on learning.**

Instructions for Use:

WARM-UP (STUDENT PAGES):

- Use this as a weekly warm-up and do one revising question each day (Monday - Friday).

- In the beginning, model questions for the students. Next, they can answer them in pairs or groups, share answers, and discuss/check.

- You could do **seven weeks of revising warm-ups** followed by **seven weeks of editing warm-ups**, or you could alternate **one week of revising warm- ups** and **one week of editing warm-ups**.

- There are **14 weeks** of daily revising and editing warm-up questions.

- Have each student write in their own workbook.

- You could also use the warm-up as a **shortened assignment.**

PRACTICE (STUDENT PAGES):

- **Teacher Table/Small Group/Tutoring** - Have students do the workbook practice pages at your teacher table while you coach and guide. Give more support to students who need it and more independence to advanced students, providing them with regular feedback.

- **Whole Group** - Another option is to complete the questions as a class. Have students justify their answers in groups and explain why their choices improve the writing. Then, remind them to apply those choices to their own compositions.

- **Station/Assignment/Practice** - Assign students the workbook practice pages as a station independently or with a buddy/group. You can check their answers or provide an answer key for self-checking.

Part 1: Revising

Revising Strategies

Warm-Up #1: Free Enterprise System
Practice #1: Planting Profits

Warm-Up #2: Wired to Wireless
Practice #2: Small Town, Big Changes

Warm-Up #3: Sam Houston: A Hero on Horseback
Practice #3: Discovering Texas

Warm-Up #4: The Flute's Sound Energy
Practice #4: Exploring Energy: Claudia's Science Journey

Warm-Up #5: Surviving the Elements
Practice #5: Texas Weather Wisdom

Warm-Up #6: San Antonio's Past and Present
Practice #6: Riveras on the Road

Warm-Up #7: Guide to the Mountains of West Texas
Practice #7: From Peaks to Prairies

Revising Strategies:

- ☑ Highlight the key words in the question.
- ☑ Highlight the sentence or paragraph in the passage.
- ☑ Read the sentence/paragraph out loud (or use a whisper phone).
- ☑ Try each answer choice.
- ☑ Eliminate/cross out answers that do not make sense.
- ☑ Choose the answer that makes the most sense.
- ☑ Lastly, justify your answer!

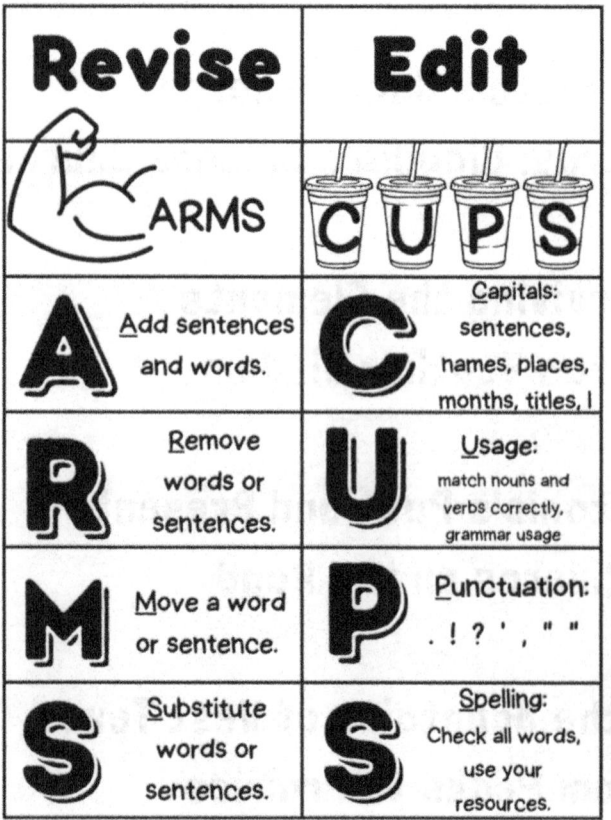

What is REVISING?

- Revising is the **effectiveness** of your writing. Is it **effective**?

- Revising is **a**dding, **r**emoving, **m**oving, or **s**ubstituting words or sentences to make your writing **BETTER**!

- Revising is **reviewing** and **improving** your writing!

REVISING: WARM-UP #1

Blake wrote a short essay about the free enterprise system. Read the essay and see what revisions he should make. Then answer the questions that follow.

Free Enterprise System

(1) The free enterprise system offers many benefits. (2) They are important.

Choice
(3) In a free enterprise system, you have a wide variety of products to choose from. (4) Many different companies make all sorts of products, so you can pick the ones you like the most. (5) This makes companies work hard to make better stuff and lower their prices. (6) It means you can choose your favorite items.

Opportunity
(7) The free enterprise system allows people to start their own businesses. (8) So, you can begin your own business and create new products or services. (9) This helps to create new jobs and improve our communities. (10) It also encourages people to think up new ideas and inventions, like fun video games or helpful apps.

(11) For example, think about all the delicious ice cream flavors at your local ice cream shop. (12) Each shop can make unique flavors, and that's because of the free enterprise system. (13) It also helps small businesses, like a lemonade stand. (14) Kids can start their own stands.

(15) So, the free enterprise system gives us plenty of choices and chances. (16) It makes our lives more interesting. (17) It makes our lives full of possibilities.

 Which sentence should replace sentence 2 to **BEST** state the central idea of this paper?

(1) The free enterprise system offers many benefits. **(2) They are important.**

A) There are many benefits within the free enterprise system.
B) My name is Blake, and I'm going to tell you all about the free enterprise system.
C) Two of the biggest benefits of the free enterprise system are choice and opportunity.
D) A person could make ice cream, or they could open a lemonade stand.

© Carlin Liborio

 The meaning of sentence 5 is unclear. What word should replace **stuff** in this sentence?

(5) This makes companies work hard to make better

A) prices
B) companies
C) products
D) snacks

and lower their prices.

 Blake wants a more effective transition between sentence 7 and sentence 8. Select the **ONE** correct phrase that should replace **So** in sentence 8 to improve this transition.

(8)
A) While the community isn't watching,
B) When you want to lose money,
C) Because it's not so easy,
D) If you have a great idea,

you can begin your own business and create new products or services.

 Which sentence would **BEST** follow and support sentence 14?

(11) For example, think about all the delicious ice cream flavors at your local ice cream shop. (12) Each shop can make unique flavors, and that's because of the free enterprise system. (13) It also helps small businesses, like a lemonade stand. (14) Kids can start their own stands.

A) This shows that anyone can do something if they want to.
B) It's a business every person should definitely try!
C) More lemonade could be sold on hot, summer days.
D) They can sell tasty drinks and learn about running a business.

 Blake wants to combine the ideas in sentence 16 and sentence 17. In the space provided, write a new sentence that combines these ideas in a clear and effective way.

(16) It makes our lives more interesting. (17) It makes our lives full of possibilities.

_____
_____

REVISING: PRACTICE #1

Sasha wrote a realistic fiction story to explain the free enterprise system. Read her story and see what revisions she should make. Then answer the questions that follow.

Planting Profits

(1) Ashley was a young girl who dreamed big. (2) She often thought about starting her own business. (3) She really wanted to.

(4) Ashley had always been interested in plants and flowers. (5) One summer, she ran a lemonade stand. (6) She had a green thumb and could make any plant grow. (7) She decided to turn her passion into a business. (8) She carefully selected different kinds of potted plants, flowers, and even some vegetables. (9) Then, she placed them on a wooden cart in front of her house with a sign that read, "Ashley's Garden - Plants and Flowers for Your Home."

(10) Next, neighbors stopped to admire Ashley's plants. (11) She greeted each customer with a warm smile. (12) She shared her knowledge about taking care of the plants. (13) People happily bought her plants. (14) They understood that Ashley's passion and care would ensure the plants grew well in their own homes.

(15) Ashley was careful in managing her expenses. (16) Her expenses included the cost of pots, soil, seeds, and her time spent tending to the plants. (17) She also learned about pricing her products to cover her costs, while also making something extra.

(18) Later, more and more people wanted to purchase her products. (19) Ashley noticed that demand was higher than she had expected. (20) To meet the demand, she increased her prices slightly. (21) They were happy to keep supporting her business.

(22) Ashley noticed that a friend from school, Conner, had started his own plant business a few houses down the street. (23) Conner's plants were also healthy and green. (24) He priced them lower than Ashley's. (25) Ashley worried that her business might go down and knew that she needed to be creative. (26) As a result, she began offering services like plant care advice.

(continued on next page)

REVISING: PRACTICE #1

Planting Profits
(continued)

(27) Big things happened. (28) She learned that in a free enterprise system, anyone could start a business, set prices, compete, and be creative. (29) She also understood that customers had choices. (30) It was important to provide them with high-quality products and excellent service.

(31) Then, Ashley's and Conner's plant businesses both grew. (32) They became friends. (33) They shared gardening tips and ideas. (34) They realized that competition encouraged them to work harder and come up with new ideas to serve their community better.

(35) How the free enterprise system worked was shown by Ashley's gardening and plant business. (36) She learned that it was about people having the freedom to start their own businesses, set prices, compete, and be creative. (37) Through her plant business, she discovered the valuable lessons of hard work. (38) These lessons would stay with her as she grew up. (39) Ashley's business continued to grow for many years.

PRACTICE #1 QUESTIONS

#1 Which sentence should replace sentence 3 to **BEST** state the central idea of this paper?

(1) Ashley was a young girl who dreamed big. (2) She often thought about starting her own business. **(3) She really wanted to.**

A) She was only 11 years old and had a brother and a sister.
B) She wanted to start a little gardening and plant business.
C) Spring is a great time to grow plants and start a business.
D) People like to use plants as decorations in their homes.

#2 Sasha has included a sentence that does not belong in the second paragraph (sentences 4-9) Which sentence should she remove?

(4) Ashley had always been interested in plants and flowers. (5) One summer, she ran a lemonade stand. (6) She had a green thumb and could make any plant grow. (7) She decided to turn her passion into a business. (8) She carefully selected different kinds of potted plants, flowers, and even some vegetables. (9) Then, she placed them on a wooden cart in front of her house with a sign that read, "Ashley's Garden - Plants and Flowers for Your Home."

A) Sentence 4
B) Sentence 5
C) Sentence 6
D) Sentence 7

#3 Sasha wants a more effective transition between the second paragraph (sentences 4-9) and the third paragraph (sentences 10-14). Select the **ONE** correct phrase that should replace **Next** in sentence 10 to improve this transition.

(10)
A) When the plants all died,
B) While they were resting,
C) Because Ashley was curious,
D) After a few days,

neighbors stopped to admire Ashley's plants.

 **#4** The meaning of sentence 17 is unclear. What phrase should replace **something extra** in this sentence?

(17) She also learned about pricing her products to cover her costs, while also making

A) soil and seeds.
B) a second business.
C) a profit.
D) a mess.

 #5 Sasha wants a more effective transition between the fourth paragraph (sentences 15-17) and the fifth paragraph (sentences 18-21). Select the **ONE** correct phrase that should replace **Later** in sentence 18 to improve this transition.

(18)
A) As word about Ashley's plant business spread,
B) Because they didn't have money,
C) While they were looking at their phones,
D) Since her plants were so expensive,

more and more people wanted to purchase her products.

 #6 The word They is not the right word for sentence 21. Which phrase should replace **They** in this sentence?

(21)
A) Her loyal customers
B) All of the plants
C) The demands
D) Conner and his family

were happy to keep supporting her business.

 #7 Which sentence would **BEST** follow and support sentence 26?

(22) Ashley noticed that a friend from school, Conner, had started his own plant business a few houses down the street. (23) Conner's plants were also healthy and green. (24) He priced them lower than Ashley's. (25) Ashley worried that her business might go down and knew that she needed to be creative. (26) As a result, she began offering services like plant care advice.

A) She knew that she had to be creative.
B) She had to find a way to get back at Conner.
C) This idea made her happy.
D) This attracted even more customers.

#8 Sasha needs a better topic sentence for the seventh paragraph (sentences 27-30). Which sentence should replace sentence 27?

(27) Big things happened. (28) She learned that in a free enterprise system, anyone could start a business, set prices, compete, and be creative. (29) She also understood that customers had choices. (30) It was important to provide them with high-quality products and excellent service.

A) Ashley learned that it was important to give her customers high-quality plants.
B) Ashley's plant business taught her lessons about competition and customer service.
C) Ashley learned a lot about keeping her plants alive and healthy.
D) Even though they each had separate businesses, Ashley and Conner became close friends.

#9 Sasha wants a more effective transition between the seventh paragraph (sentences 27-30) and the eighth paragraph (sentences 31-34). Select the **ONE** correct phrase that should replace **Then** in sentence 31 to improve this transition.

(31)
A) The very next minute,
B) Because they didn't care,
C) As the summer went on,
D) While she was dreaming,

Ashley's and Conner's plant businesses both grew.

#10 Sentence 35 needs to be revised. In the space provided, rewrite sentence 35 in a clear and effective way.

(35) How the free enterprise system worked was shown by Ashley's gardening and plant business.

_____
_____
_____

REVISING: WARM-UP #2

Elia wrote an essay summarizing technological changes in communication. Read her essay and see what revisions she should make. Then answer the questions that follow.

Wired to Wireless

(1) Over the last century and a half, technological advances have caused huge changes in communication. (2) The telegraph was invented in the 19th century. (3) It improved long-distance communication by transmitting Morse code messages over wires.

(4) The telephone, developed by Alexander Graham Bell in 1876, brought real-time voice communication to everyone. (5) It connected people across great distances. (6) It changed the ways we communicate. (7) Telephones went from analog landlines to digital networks.

(8) Then, the introduction of computers and the internet has brought a new era of communication. (9) Computers allow individuals to send emails, create digital documents, and participate in video conferencing. (10) The internet has connected billions of people and devices worldwide. (11) It allows for instant messaging and social media. (12) It allows for access to information.

(13) These technological changes have changed communication from a slow process to an instant activity. (14) They influence every part of modern life, from personal relationships to business and global communication.

 Which sentence would **BEST** follow and support sentence 3?

(1) Over the last century and a half, technological advances have caused huge changes in communication. (2) The telegraph was invented in the 19th century. (3) It improved long-distance communication by transmitting Morse code messages over wires.

A) This invention changed communication rapidly.
B) The code was transmitted over wires.
C) The smoke signal was one of the oldest forms of long-distance communication.
D) Another form of early long-distance communication was drumming.

#2 Elia wants to combine the ideas in sentences 5 and 6. In the box provided, write a new sentence that combines these ideas in a clear and effective way.

(5) It connected people across great distances. (6) It changed the ways we communicate.

_____
_____

#3 The meaning of sentence 7 is unclear. What word should replace **went** in this sentence?

(7) Telephones
A) gone
B) arrived
C) stayed
D) developed
from analog landlines to digital networks.

#4 Elia wants a more effective transition between the second paragraph (sentences 4-7) and the third paragraph (sentences 8-12). Select the **ONE** correct phrase that should replace **Then** in sentence 8 to improve this transition.

(8)
A) At that very moment,
B) In recent years,
C) From time to time,
D) Since the beginning of time,
the introduction of computers and the internet has brought a new era of communication.

#5 Elia wants to combine the ideas in sentences 11 and 12. In the box provided, write a new sentence that combines these ideas clearly and effectively.

(11) It allows for instant messaging and social media. (12) It allows for access to information.

_____
_____

REVISING: PRACTICE #2

Martin wrote a realistic fiction story to explain his understanding of the effects of technological changes. Read his story and see what revisions he should make. Then answer the questions that follow.

Small Town, Big Changes

(1) Izzy and Daniel had been best friends for as long as they could remember. (2) They lived on opposite sides of a small town in Texas. (3) Every day, they would meet at the park to play and have fun.

(4) Something happened. (5) A brand-new highway was built right through the middle of their town. (6) It was wider and smoother than any road they had ever seen. (7) This highway was part of a huge network of roads and bridges connecting towns. (8) It was an amazing system of transportation.

(9) With this new highway, things started to change. (10) Izzy's father, who worked in a nearby town, could now reach his workplace in half the time it used to take. (11) He was home earlier in the evenings. (12) The family had more time to spend together. (13) Daniel's mom started an online business selling her homemade crafts. (14) Although she could have shipped her products before, the new highway made it faster and more convenient to send orders across the state.

(15) As for Izzy and Daniel, the new highway made it easier for them to meet and play at the park. (16) Daniel's parents could drop him off at the park on their way to work. (17) They could pick her up after work. (18) Izzy and Daniel also discovered that the park had free Wi-Fi. (19) It allowed them to look up exciting new games. (20) It also allowed them to chat with friends from far-away places.

(21) Then Izzy and Daniel met a new kid named Carlos. (22) He had just moved to their town with his family. (23) They had chosen this town because of its easy access to the highway. (24) Carlos' dad worked in the city, and the highway allowed him to commute quickly. (25) Carlos' mom, a chef, had her own catering business, which she advertised online. (26) In several nearby towns already, events she had catered.

(Continued on next page)

REVISING: PRACTICE #2

Small Town, Big Changes (continued)

(27) The kids changed. (28) They learned about each other's different backgrounds and cultures. (29) They enjoyed Carlos' mom's delicious food. (30) Carlos introduced them to his friends from other towns through online gaming. (31) Soon, they had friends from all over the state of Texas.

(32) The changes in transportation and communication brought Izzy, Daniel, and Carlos together. (33) The changes also made their small town more connected to the rest of the world.

(34) Years passed, and the three friends decided to go on a road trip to visit the places they had heard or read about. (35) They went on an adventure, using the same highways that had brought them together in the first place. (36) As they went, they were amazed at how technology had changed their lives and their world.

(37) Technological changes in transportation and communication led to more interdependence among individuals, communities, and the world. (38) As a result of these advancements, the world became smaller and more interconnected. (39) In many ways, the lives of people like Izzy, Daniel, and Carlos improved in many ways.

PRACTICE #2 QUESTIONS

#1 Martin needs a better topic sentence for the second paragraph (sentences 4-8). Which sentence should replace sentence 4?

(4) Something happened. (5) A brand-new highway was built right through the middle of their town. (6) It was wider and smoother than any road they had ever seen. (7) This highway was part of a huge network of roads and bridges connecting towns. (8) It was an amazing system of transportation.

A) The town they lived in was very small.
B) In fact, playing in the park was their favorite thing to do.
C) You'll never guess what happened next.
D) One day, their small town experienced a big change.

#2 Martin wants to combine the ideas in sentences 11 and 12. In the box provided, write a new sentence that combines these ideas clearly and effectively.

(11) He was home earlier in the evenings. (12) The family had more time to spend together.

#3 The meaning of sentence 17 is unclear. What phrase should replace **They** in this sentence?

(17)
A) Izzy and Daniel
B) Daniel's mom's customers
C) Friends from far-off places
D) Izzy's parents
 could pick her up after work.

 Martin wants to combine the ideas in sentences 19 and 20. In the box provided, write a new sentence that combines these ideas in a clear and effective way.

(19) It allowed them to look up exciting new games. (20) It also allowed them to chat with friends from far-away places.

_____
_____
_____

 Martin wants a more effective transition between the fourth paragraph (sentences 15-20) and the fifth paragraph (sentences 21-26). Select the **ONE** correct phrase that should replace **Then** in sentence 21 to improve this transition.

(21)
A) While playing at the park one day,
B) Before meeting the new kid,
C) Because they were so lonely,
D) While traveling on the new highway,

Izzy and Daniel met a new kid named Carlos.

 What is the **BEST** way to revise sentence 26?

(26) In several nearby towns already, events she had catered.

A) Already in several nearby towns she had catered events.
B) She had already catered events in several nearby towns.
C) In several already nearby towns she had catered events.
D) She had catered events in nearby several towns already.

 Martin needs a better topic sentence for the sixth paragraph (sentences 27-31). Which sentence should replace sentence 27?

(27) The kids changed. (28) They learned about each other's different backgrounds and cultures. (29) They enjoyed Carlos' mom's delicious food. (30) Carlos introduced them to his friends from other towns through online gaming. (31) Soon, they had friends from all over the state of Texas.

A) Izzy and Daniel met Carlos' family.
B) Thanks to the new highway, there was so much to do.
C) Izzy, Daniel, and Carlos quickly became friends.
D) Carlos was a shy kid at first.

#8 Which sentence would **BEST** follow and support sentence 33?

(32) The changes in transportation and communication brought Izzy, Daniel, and Carlos together. (33) The changes also made their small town more connected to the rest of the world.

A) The kids realized that the rest of the world was no longer as big and far away as it once seemed.
B) The changes just went on and on and almost never stopped.
C) This was all because of the changes in transportation and communication.
D) All these changes made the kids a little anxious.

#9 The meaning of sentence 36 is unclear. What word should replace **went** in this sentence?

(36) As they
A) walked,
B) flew,
C) traveled,
D) left,
they were amazed at how technology had changed their lives and their world.

#10 Sentence 39 repeats information. In the box provided, rewrite this sentence in a clear and effective way.

(39) In many ways, the lives of people like Izzy, Daniel, and Carlos improved in many ways.

_____

REVISING: WARM-UP #3

Daniel wrote a short essay about the Sam Houston Monument. Read the essay and see what revisions he should make. Then answer the questions that follow.

Sam Houston: A Hero on Horseback

(1) In Houston, Texas, stands a towering monument. (2) This monument honors a legendary person named General Sam Houston. (3) This magnificent statue was finished in 1925. (4) It honors General Houston's leadership and dedication to Texas' independence.

(5) Created by Italian artist Enrico Cerracchio, the bronze sculpture shows General Houston riding his faithful horse. (6) With a determined expression and outstretched arm, General Houston's statue captures his determination in leading Texas to victory at the Battle of San Jacinto. (7) The shape of his cape and the strong muscles of his horse make it look as if the statue is moving with power.

(8) More than just a work of art it is. (9) The Sam Houston Monument is an important historical symbol. (10) It reminds us of General Houston's contributions to Texas' history. (11) His courage, strength, and dedication to the cause of freedom continue to inspire generations of Texans.

(12) Now, the Sam Houston Monument stands as an admired landmark in Houston, attracting visitors from around the world. (13) It serves as a symbol of inspiration, reminding us of the spirit of a man who shaped the state of Texas.

 Which is the **BEST** way to combine sentences 1 and 2?

> (1) In Houston, Texas, stands a towering monument. (2) This monument honors a legendary person named General Sam Houston.

A) In Houston, Texas, stands a towering monument that honors a legendary person named General Sam Houston.
B) In Houston, Texas, stands a towering monument, but this monument honors a legendary person named General Sam Houston.
C) Because in Houston, Texas, stands a towering monument, this monument honors a legendary person named General Sam Houston.
D) Although in Houston, Texas, stands a towering monument, this monument honors a legendary person named General Sam Houston.

#2 The meaning of sentence 7 is unclear. What phrase should replace **it** in this sentence?

(7) The shape of his cape and the strong muscles of his horse make

A) the battle
B) the artist
C) the statue
D) the victory

look as if it is moving with power.

#3 In the box provided, revise sentence 8 in a clear and effective way.

(8) More than just a work of art it is.

_____
_____

#4 Daniel wants a more effective transition between the third paragraph (sentences 8-11) and the fourth paragraph (sentences 12-13). Select the **ONE** correct phrase in sentence 12 to improve this transition.

(12)
A) After a few weeks,
B) In the first place,
C) To this day,
D) In the future,

the Sam Houston Monument stands as an admired landmark in Houston, attracting visitors from around the world.

#5 Which sentence would **BEST** follow and support sentence 13 and conclude the essay?

(13) It serves as a symbol of inspiration, reminding us of the spirit of a man who shaped the State of Texas.

A) There are many other monuments located throughout the state of Texas.
B) Houston did so much to shape the state of Texas.
C) This monument is located in downtown Houston.
D) His legacy continues to inspire pride in the hearts of Texans.

REVISING: PRACTICE #3

Robert wrote a realistic fiction story to explain his understanding of the meaning of symbols and landmarks of Texas. Read his story and see what revisions he should make. Then answer the questions that follow.

Discovering Texas

(1) Stefan lived in the heart of Texas, and he was a curious 4th grader. (2) He was always full of questions and loved learning about the history of his home state.

(3) Stefan did something. (4) He was able to choose the topic of his project. (5) He was interested in the six flags that had flown over Texas - the flags of Spain, France, Mexico, the Republic of Texas, the United States, and the Confederate States.

(6) His adventure began at the San Jacinto Monument. (7) It's a tall structure that honors the Battle of San Jacinto. (8) This battle was a very important one for Texas' freedom from Mexico. (9) Stefan learned about the brave soldiers who fought there. (10) He felt proud to know about this important part of Texas history.

(11) He then visited the historic Alamo, where he could feel the history in the air. (12) The Alamo was a symbol of bravery and sacrifice. (13) Stefan learned about those who stood against Santa Anna's army and made a big sacrifice. (14) A lasting mark they left on Texas history.

(15) Stefan needed more. (16) The Spanish flag stood for the time when Spain colonized Texas and established San Antonio. (17) The French flag represented a brief period of French rule in the area. (18) The Mexican flag showed the time when Texas was a part of Mexico and its rich culture and traditions.

(19) The Republic of Texas flag reminded Stefan of the time Texas declared itself a separate nation. (20) The United States flag highlighted Texas becoming a state. (21) The German flag is not one that flew over Texas. (22) The Confederate flag was from a tough time in the country's history. (23) It was also a part of Texas' past during the Civil War era.

(24) Learning about these symbols and landmarks made Stefan see that Texas was like a quilt, made up of different threads of history, bravery, and strength. (25) Each flag and landmark had a story of hardship and victory. (26) Each flag and landmark had a story of the fight for freedom.

(27) Then, Stefan's love for Texas history continued to grow. (28) He shared what he had learned with friends and family.

(29) In the end, Stefan realized these symbols and landmarks are not just old things from history books. (30) They are reminders of the spirit and identity of Texas. (31) They show the struggles and victories that built Texas' legacy and the dedication to freedom that defined the state he was so proud to call home.

PRACTICE #3 QUESTIONS

#1 Which sentence should replace sentence 3 to **BEST** state the central idea of this paper?

(1) Stefan lived in the heart of Texas, and he was a curious 4th grader. (2) He was always full of questions and loved learning about the history of his home state.

(3) Stefan did something. (4) He was able to choose the topic of his project.

A) Stefan always got good grades, especially in social studies.
B) One year, Stefan read a book about Texas history for fun.
C) One year, Stefan had a school project about Texas history.
D) Stefan really wanted to impress his friends and family.

#2 Which sentence would **BEST** follow and support sentence 5?

(5) He was interested in the six flags that had flown over Texas - the flags of Spain, France, Mexico, the Republic of Texas, the United States, and the Confederate States.

A) Stefan dreaded the idea of having to do a summer project.
B) He was really interested in the history of those flags.
C) He had a hard time deciding on a topic for his project.
D) He was excited to explore and understand their meanings.

#3 What is the **BEST** way to combine sentences 9 and 10?

(9) Stefan learned about the brave soldiers who fought there. (10) He felt proud to know about this important part of Texas history.

A) Stefan learned about the brave soldiers who fought there, he felt proud to know about this important part of Texas history.
B) Stefan learned about the brave soldiers who fought there and felt proud to know about this important part of Texas history.
C) Stefan learned about the brave soldiers who fought there because he felt proud to know about this important part of Texas history.
D) Stefan learned about the brave soldiers who fought there, yet he felt proud to know about this important part of Texas history.

30 © Carlin Liborio

 **#4** The meaning of sentence 13 is unclear. What phrase should replace **those** in this sentence?

(13) Stefan learned about [A) Stefan's classmates / B) Santa Anna's army / C) the defenders / D) the six flags] who stood against Santa Anna's army and made a big sacrifice.

A) Stefan's classmates
B) Santa Anna's army
C) the defenders
D) the six flags

 #5 In the box provided, revise sentence 14 in a clear and effective way.

(14) A lasting mark they left on Texas history.

 **#6** Robert needs a better topic sentence for the fifth paragraph (sentences 15-18). Which sentence should replace sentence 15?

(15) Stefan needed more. (16) The Spanish flag stood for the time when Spain colonized Texas and established San Antonio. (17) The French flag represented a brief period of French rule in the area. (18) The Mexican flag showed the time Texas was a part of Mexico and its rich culture and traditions.

A) Stefan spent his entire summer vacation working on the project.
B) Stefan wanted to know more about the stories of the flags that represented Texas.
C) Studying the different flags made Stefan wish he could travel to Spain and France.
D) The Texas State Capitol is located in downtown Austin, Texas.

 **#7** Robert has included a sentence that does not belong in the sixth paragraph (sentences 19-23) Which sentence should he remove?

(19) The Republic of Texas flag reminded Stefan of the time Texas declared itself a separate nation. (20) The United States flag highlighted Texas becoming a state. (21) The German flag is not one that flew over Texas. (22) The Confederate flag was from a tough time in the country's history. (23) It was also a part of Texas' past during the Civil War era.

A) Sentence 19
B) Sentence 20
C) Sentence 21
D) Sentence 22

#8 Robert wants to combine the ideas in sentences 25 and 26. In the box provided, write a new sentence that combines these ideas in a clear and effective way.

(25) Each flag and landmark had a story of hardship and victory. (26) Each flag and landmark had a story of the fight for freedom.

_____

_____

_____

#9 Robert wants a more effective transition between the seventh paragraph (sentences 24-26) and the eighth paragraph (sentences 27-28). Select the **ONE** correct phrase that should replace **Then** in sentence 27 to improve this transition.

(27)
A) While his love of history grew,
B) Besides working on his project,
C) After finishing his school project,
D) Before he was sharing what he had learned,

Stefan's love for Texas history continued to grow.

#10 Which sentence would **BEST** follow and support sentence 28?

(28) He shared what he had learned with friends and family.

A) This made them curious and inspired them to explore Texas' amazing history too.
B) All of this information about Texas only confused them.
C) Stefan began to doubt his own hard work.
D) Stefan's mom's favorite part of the project was the part about the French flag.

REVISING: WARM-UP #4

Marco wrote a short essay about the sound energy created by the flute. Read the essay and see what revisions he should make. Then answer the questions that follow.

The Flute's Sound Energy

(1) The flute is a beautiful musical instrument. (2) It represents sound energy in action. (3) Sound energy is the vibration of particles. (4) The flute uses this energy to produce tunes.

(5) Blows air across the flute's hole when a flutist, it vibrates the air inside the instrument. (6) This vibration travels through the body of the flute, changing the air particles. (7) These vibrations create sound waves that travel through the air. (8) There, they are interpreted by our brains as the thing we hear.

(9) The design of the flute is important to its ability to make different pitches and tones. (10) The size of the finger holes and the length of the flute determine the frequencies of the vibrations and the notes we hear. (11) A skilled flutist can create a wide range of sounds.

(12) In addition, the flute changes energy from one form to another. (13) The player's breath is a source of kinetic energy, which sets the air inside the flute in motion and produces sound energy. (14) As the flute is played, it demonstrates how kinetic energy is transformed into sound energy.

 Which is the **BEST** way to combine sentences 3 and 4?

> (3) Sound energy is the vibration of particles. (4) The flute uses this energy to produce tunes.

A) Sound energy is the vibration of particles, but the flute uses this energy to produce tunes.
B) Sound energy is the vibration of particles, and the flute uses this energy to produce tunes.
C) Sound energy is the vibration of particles because the flute uses this energy to produce tunes.
D) Sound energy is the vibration of particles, or the flute uses this energy to produce tunes.

#2 What is the **BEST** revision to make in sentence 5?

(5) Blows air across the flute's hole when a flutist, it vibrates the air inside the instrument.

A) When a flutist blows air across the flute's hole, the air inside the instrument vibrates.
B) When the flute's hole blows air across the flutist, it vibrates the air inside the instrument.
C) When a flutist blows air across the flute's hole, vibrates the air inside the instrument it does.
D) When vibrating the air across the flute's hole a flutist blows air inside the instrument.

#3 The meaning of sentence 8 is unclear. What word should replace **thing** in this sentence?

(7) These vibrations create sound waves that travel through the air. (8) There, they are interpreted by our brains as the ⟨ A) waves B) vibration C) ear D) sound ⟩ we hear.

#4 Which sentence would **BEST** follow and support sentence 11?

(9) The design of the flute is important to its ability to make different pitches and tones. (10) The size of the finger holes and the length of the flute determine the frequencies of the vibrations and the notes we hear. (11) A skilled flutist can create a wide range of sounds.

A) The flute is one of the most beautiful musical instruments.
B) This shows the power of sound energy.
C) Becoming a skilled flutist can take years of practice.
D) This works the same way with other instruments.

#5 Which sentence would **BEST** follow and support sentence 14 to conclude this essay?

(12) In addition, the flute changes energy from one form to another. (13) The player's breath is a source of kinetic energy, which sets the air inside the flute in motion and produces sound energy. (14) As the flute is played, it demonstrates how kinetic energy is transformed into sound energy.

A) In conclusion, light energy is even more interesting than sound energy.
B) This all starts with the flutist's breath.
C) In conclusion, this process shows how musical instruments like the flute rely on energy transformations to create sound.
D) To sum it up, I hope you enjoyed my short essay about sound energy.

REVISING: PRACTICE #4

Julia wrote a realistic fiction story to explain her understanding of the forms of energy she studied in science class. Read her story and see what revisions she should make. Then answer the questions that follow.

Exploring Energy: Claudia's Science Journey

(1) At ten years old, Claudia loved science. (2) She enjoyed learning the secrets of how things worked. (3) She studied them. (4) Claudia became interested in science during a visit to a science museum. (5) While there, she saw exhibits that explained mechanical, sound, electrical, light, and thermal energies.

(6) To begin with, mechanical energy sparked Claudia's curiosity, to begin with. (7) Mechanical energy is the energy of movement and position. (8) She experimented with a pendulum, observing how potential energy transformed into kinetic energy.

(9) There's more. (10) Claudia, a music lover, discovered how vibrations create different sound frequencies. (11) By experimenting with different materials, she learned about the transmission of sound energy.

(12) Following that, she studied it. (13) Claudia explored circuits and the flow of electrons. (14) She learned how electrical energy powers many devices in everyday life. (15) She also learned about the importance of conductors and insulators.

(16) The characteristics of light energy fascinated Claudia. (17) She explored the spectrum of light and understood light's behaviors, such as reflection and refraction. (18) She learned how light travels and changes. (19) Her favorite color is purple.

(20) Thermal energy, the energy of heat, was another type of energy she investigated. (21) Claudia explored the movement of atoms and molecules within objects that generated heat. (22) She tested different materials for their heat conduction and insulation properties. (23) Helped her it did to understand how temperature affects matter.

(24) Next, she started seeing examples of energy everywhere around her. (25) The swings at the playground showed mechanical energy. (26) The kitchen stove used thermal energy to cook. (27) She recognized how different energies act in everyday life.

(28) The more Claudia learned about these different forms of energy, the more she wanted to know. (29) The mysterious concepts became clearer, opening up a new world of understanding for her.

PRACTICE #4 QUESTIONS

Which sentence should replace sentence 3 to **BEST** state the central idea of this paper?

(1) At ten years old, Claudia loved science. (2) She enjoyed learning the secrets of how things worked. **(3) She studied them.** (4) Claudia became interested in science during a visit to a science museum. (5) While there, she saw exhibits that explained mechanical, sound, electrical, light, and thermal energies.

A) Science was always Julia's favorite subject.
B) Claudia went to a local science museum.
C) She has been to many different museums in her area.
D) She especially liked exploring the different forms of energy.

Sentence 6 repeats information. In the box provided, revise this sentence in a clear and effective way.

(6) To begin with, mechanical energy sparked Claudia's curiosity, to begin with.

_____
_____

Which sentence would **BEST** follow and support sentence 8?

(6) To begin with, mechanical energy sparked Claudia's curiosity, to begin with. (7) Mechanical energy is the energy of movement and position. (8) She experimented with a pendulum, observing how potential energy transformed into kinetic energy.

A) This hands-on experience taught her that energy could change forms.
B) The pendulum experiment was so interesting!
C) Claudia learned many different things by doing this experiment.
D) Mechanical energy was the first type of energy that she studied.

Julia needs a better topic sentence for the third paragraph (sentences 9-11). Which sentence should replace sentence 9?

(9) There's more. (10) Claudia, a music lover, discovered how vibrations create different sound frequencies. (11) By experimenting with different materials, she learned about the transmission of sound energy.

A) She couldn't wait to see what came next.
B) Claudia was a music lover.
C) There was still so much to learn about forms of energy.
D) Sound energy was another interesting idea.

#5 The meaning of sentence 12 is unclear. What word should replace **it** in this sentence?

(12) Following that, she studied

A) music.
B) energy.
C) electricity.
D) sound.

#6 In the box provided, combine the ideas in sentences 14 and 15 in a clear and effective way.

(14) She learned how electrical energy powers many devices in everyday life. (15) She also learned about the importance of conductors and insulators.

_____

#7 Julia has included a sentence that does not belong in the fifth paragraph (sentences 16-19). Which sentence should she remove?

(16) The characteristics of light energy fascinated Claudia. (17) She explored the spectrum of light and understood light's behaviors, such as reflection and refraction. (18) She learned how light travels and changes. (19) Her favorite color is purple.

A) Sentence 16
B) Sentence 17
C) Sentence 18
D) Sentence 19

 **#8** What is the **BEST** revision to make in sentence 23?

(23) Helped her it did to understand how temperature affects matter.

A) How temperature affects matter helped her to understand it.
B) It helped her to understand how temperature affects matter.
C) Understanding how temperature affects matter, it helped her.
D) Understanding it helped her how temperature affects matter.

 **#9** Julia wants a more effective transition between the sixth paragraph (sentences 20-23) and the seventh paragraph (sentences 24-27). Select the **ONE** correct phrase that should replace **Next** in sentence 24 to improve this transition.

(24)
A) Before Claudia forgot,
B) Although she had learned a lot,
C) As Claudia learned more,
D) Because there was so much Claudia didn't know,

she started seeing examples of energy everywhere around her.

 **#10** Which sentence would **BEST** follow and support sentence 29 to conclude this story?

(28) The more Claudia learned about these different forms of energy, the more she wanted to know. (29) The mysterious concepts became clearer, opening up a new world of understanding for her.

A) That's everything that Claudia learned about the different forms of energy.
B) She also understands exactly how the water cycle works.
C) The idea of sound energy was the easiest for Claudia to understand.
D) Her mind now saw connections between what she had learned and the real world.

REVISING: WARM-UP #5

Phillip wrote a short story. Read the story and see what revisions he should make. Then answer the questions that follow.

Surviving the Elements

(1) The Perez family went on a weekend camping trip, looking to have some fun in nature. (2) As they set up their tent near a lovely lake, the sky suddenly darkened. (3) Something bad happened. (4) In a panic, the Perez family quickly gathered their belongings to secure their campsite before the storm hit.

(5) Got stronger the storm quickly. (6) It turned the peaceful setting into chaos. (7) Lightning flashed in the sky, and thunder echoed through the forest. (8) The Perez family huddled in their tent, seeking cover from the endless downpour. (9) Water pooled around them as the ground struggled to absorb the flood.

(10) Then, the family came together. (11) They shared stories and laughter, trying to ease the tension. (12) The storm raged on throughout the night, testing their toughness. (13) At dawn, the storm passed, revealing a changed landscape. (14) The once-peaceful campsite was now covered with stuff.

(15) As they came out of the battered tent, the Perez family was amazed by the power of nature and their own endurance. (16) Despite the unexpected challenge, the family had grown closer. (17) Their experience became a tale to be retold around future campfires.

 Which sentence should replace sentence 3 to **BEST** state the central idea of this paper?

(2) As they set up their tent near a lovely lake, the sky suddenly darkened.
(3) Something bad happened. (4) In a panic, the Perez family quickly gathered their belongings to secure their campsite before the storm hit.

A) As the sky got darker, the family gathered their things.
B) The Perez family was very experienced at camping.
C) There were so many things to do at the lake once they arrived.
D) An unexpected thunderstorm rolled in with fierce winds and heavy rain.

#2 Sentence 5 needs to be revised. In the box provided revise this sentence in a clear and effective way.

(5) Got stronger the storm quickly.

_____
_____

#3 Phillip wants a more effective transition between the second paragraph (sentences 5-9) and the third paragraph (sentences 10-14). Select the **ONE** correct phrase that should replace **Then** in sentence 10 to improve this transition.

(10)
A) During the storm,
B) Unless they weren't prepared,
C) Because the storm ended,
D) While they were having fun,

the family came together.

#4 The meaning of sentence 14 is unclear. What phrase should replace **stuff** in this sentence?

(14) The once-peaceful campsite was now covered with

A) lightning and thunder.
B) night and day.
C) puddles and fallen branches.
D) stories and laughter.

#5 Which sentence would **BEST** follow and support sentence 17 to conclude this story?

(17) Their experience became a tale to be retold around future campfires.

A) The family's next camping trip was much more peaceful.
B) If they had only checked the weather forecast, none of this would have happened.
C) That's what happened during the Perez family camping trip.
D) It became a story of togetherness in the face of an unexpected storm.

REVISING: PRACTICE #5

Carolyn wrote a folktale about predicting the weather. Read her story and see what revisions she should make. Then answer the questions that follow.

⚡ Texas Weather Wisdom ⚡

(1) In the heart of the Texas Hill Country lived an old rancher named Cody. (2) He was famous for his ability to predict the weather. (3) Folks in the nearby towns often asked for his advice before planning outdoor events or starting on long journeys. (4) They said that Cody had a magical stone. (5) The stone was passed down to him through generations.

(6) Legend said that Cody's great-grandfather, an experienced cowboy, discovered the stone during a violent storm. (7) As the thunder roared and lightning flashed, the old cowboy took shelter in a cave as the thunder roared and lightning flashed. (8) There, he found a strange, smooth stone, which he carefully put in his pocket. (9) From that day on, the stone became a family treasure.

(10) Cody inherited the stone and the gift of weather prediction. (11) He understood the stone's true power was not from magic. (12) Cody's ability to predict the weather came from close observation and a deep connection to the land. (13) Then, he would go to his favorite spot on the ranch. (14) There, he would observe the vast Texas sky.

(15) To measure changes in weather, Cody used the stone's surface. (16) If the stone felt cool and damp, he predicted rain. (17) If it was warm and dry, a hot day was ahead. (18) By rubbing his fingers over the stone's texture, he guessed humidity was in the air. (19) Cody raised longhorn cattle. (20) To help predict the weather, Cody kept a thing noting the stone's condition, date, and weather patterns.

(21) Cody noticed other things. (22) When the cattle huddled close together and birds flew low, he expected a storm. (23) To the untrained eye, these signs might seem small, but not to Cody. (24) His experience in observing the animals guided him to predict it.

(25) Cody's predictions were very accurate. (26) Amazed by his skill the townsfolk were. (27) They called him the Weather Whisperer. (28) As news of Cody's abilities spread, people went to him for guidance. (29) He generously shared his knowledge.

(30) In the Texas Hill Country, Cody's life became known for the art of measuring, recording, and predicting changes in weather. (31) The mystical stone reminds us that even though technology changes, the wisdom of the land remains.

© Carlin Liborio

PRACTICE #5 QUESTIONS

 Which is the **BEST** way to combine sentences 4 and 5?

(4) They said that Cody had a magical stone. (5) The stone was passed down to him through generations.

A) They said that Cody had a magical stone the stone was passed down to him through generations.
B) They said that Cody had a magical stone, so the stone was passed down to him through generations.
C) They said that Cody had a magical stone which was passed down to him through generations.
D) Because they said that Cody had a magical stone, the stone was passed down to him through generations.

 Sentence 7 repeats information. In the box provided, revise this sentence in a clear and effective way.

(7) As the thunder roared and lightning flashed, the old cowboy took shelter in a cave as the thunder roared and lightning flashed.

_____
_____

 Carolyn wants a more effective transition between sentence 12 and sentence 13 in the third paragraph (sentences 10-14). Select the **ONE** correct phrase that should replace **Then** in sentence 13 to improve this transition.

(13)
A) Each morning,
B) When he didn't feel like it,
C) Because it was raining,
D) While people were visiting,

he would go to his favorite spot on the ranch.

 **#4** Carolyn has included a sentence that does not belong in the fourth paragraph (sentences 15-20). Which sentence should she remove?

(15) To measure changes in weather, Cody used the stone's surface. (16) If the stone felt cool and damp, he predicted rain. (17) If it was warm and dry, a hot day was ahead. (18) By rubbing his fingers over the stone's texture, he guessed humidity was in the air. (19) Cody raised longhorn cattle. (20) To record these observations, Cody carefully kept a thing where he noted the stone's condition along with the date and weather patterns.

A) Sentence 16
B) Sentence 17
C) Sentence 18
D) Sentence 19

 **#5** The meaning of sentence 20 is unclear. What word should replace **thing** in this sentence?

(20) To help predict the weather, Cody kept a [A) stone / B) weather / C) journal / D) horse] noting the stone's condition, date, and weather patterns.

 **#6** Carolyn needs a better topic sentence for the fifth paragraph (sentences 21-24). Which sentence should replace sentence 21?

(21) Cody noticed other things. (22) When the cattle huddled close together and birds flew low, he expected a storm. (23) To the untrained eye, these signs might seem small, but not to Cody. (24) His experience in observing the animals guided him to predict it.

A) By observing the stone closely, Cody could predict the weather.
B) There were so many ways that Cody could predict how the weather would be.
C) There was nothing Cody enjoyed more than predicting the weather.
D) Cody also paid close attention to the behavior of animals on his ranch.

 **#7** The meaning of sentence 24 is unclear. What phrase should replace **it** in this sentence?

(24) His experience in observing the animals guided him in predicting

A) the animals' behavior.
B) the weather.
C) his guidance.
D) careful observation.

#8 Sentence 26 needs to be revised. In the box provided revise this sentence in a clear and effective way.

(26) Amazed by his skill the townsfolk were.

___

#9 Which sentence would **BEST** follow and support sentence 29?

(29) He generously shared his knowledge.

A) He told them of the importance of careful observation and a deep respect for nature.
B) Cody also enjoyed talking about how to take care of cattle, sheep, and horses.
C) He always shared his advice whenever somebody asked.
D) Although he never complained, Cody didn't like his nickname, the Weather Whisperer.

#10 Which sentence would **BEST** follow and support sentence 31 to conclude this story?

(31) The mystical stone reminds us that even though technology changes, the wisdom of the land remains.

A) Predicting the weather can be easy if you just give it a try.
B) Another way to predict the weather is to use artificial intelligence.
C) Meteorologists study the Earth's atmosphere and weather patterns.
D) This wisdom has been passed down through generations.

REVISING: WARM-UP #6

Ramon wrote a short essay comparing the city of San Antonio's past and present. Read the essay and see what revisions he should make. Then answer the questions that follow.

San Antonio's Past and Present

(1) San Antonio is a city with a rich cultural heritage and a long history. (2) Things have happened to it. (3) Founded in 1718, the city's early years were marked by Spanish colonization, seen in landmarks like the Alamo and the Spanish Governor's Palace. (4) In the past, San Antonio thrived as a center for trade, connecting Mexico and the United States. (5) Created a unique culture the city's diverse population.

(6) Now, San Antonio is an energetic city that blends tradition with modern life. (7) The city's skyline has modern skyscrapers, reflecting economic growth and urban development. (8) The River Walk, once an ordinary waterway, has evolved into a busy tourist destination lined with restaurants, shops, and entertainment. (9) San Antonio's many cultural events, such as Fiesta, and an exciting arts scene showcase a goal to preserve and celebrate its diverse history. (10) They have so many cultural events there!

(11) There are other things. (12) They include urban overcrowding, crime, and issues of economic fairness. (13) People are trying to solve these problems. (14) As San Antonio continues to grow and change, it is a symbol of the strength of its past and the promise of a successful future.

 Which sentence should replace sentence 2 to **BEST** state the central idea of this paper?

(1) San Antonio is a city with a rich cultural heritage and a long history. **(2) Things have happened to it.** (3) Founded in 1718, the city's early years were marked by Spanish colonization, seen in landmarks like the Alamo and the Spanish Governor's Palace.

A) The city of San Antonio hasn't changed all that much over the years.
B) There are lots of activities there for kids and adults.
C) Anyone who has been to San Antonio says that they love it.
D) It has experienced many changes from its past to the present day.

#2 Sentence 5 needs to be revised. In the box provided revise this sentence in a clear and effective way.

(5) Created a unique culture the city's diverse population.

#3 Ramon wants a more effective transition between the first paragraph (sentences 1-5) and the second paragraph (sentences 6-10). Select the **ONE** correct phrase that should replace **Now** in sentence 6 to improve this transition.

(6)
A) Today,
B) Back in the day,
C) When something changed,
D) Because the city was the same,

San Antonio is an energetic city that blends tradition with modern life.

#4 Read the second paragraph (sentences 6-10) again. Which sentence in this paragraph repeats information and should be removed?

(6) Now, San Antonio stands as an energetic city that blends tradition with modern life. (7) The city's skyline has modern skyscrapers, reflecting economic growth and urban development. (8) The River Walk, once an ordinary waterway, has evolved into a busy tourist destination lined with restaurants, shops, and entertainment. (9) San Antonio's many cultural events, such as Fiesta, and an exciting arts scene showcase a goal to preserve and celebrate its diverse history. (10) They have so many cultural events there!

A) Sentence 7
B) Sentence 8
C) Sentence 9
D) Sentence 10

#5 Ramon needs a better topic sentence for the third paragraph (sentences 11-14). Which sentence should replace sentence 11?

(11) There are other things. (12) They include urban overcrowding, crime, and issues of economic fairness. (13) People are trying to solve these problems. (14) As San Antonio continue to grow and change, it is a symbol of the strength of its past and the promise of a successful future.

A) The city's cultural events are fun and interesting.
B) If the city keeps growing, it's going to be too crowded.
C) There's more to know about the city.
D) However, there are challenges.

REVISING: PRACTICE #6

Lisa wrote a story about a road trip across Texas. Read her story and see what revisions she should make. Then answer the questions that follow.

Riveras on the Road

(1) The Riveras loved to take family road trips. (2) They went somewhere together. (3) The journey began in the sun-kissed deserts of West Texas, where Midland and Odessa stood on the horizon. (4) As they crossed the dry land, the family marveled at the rhythm of the oil pump jacks and admired the spirit of these oil-rich towns.

(5) As they drive eastward, the landscape changed into rolling hills and vibrant greenery. (6) San Angelo, located along the banks of the Concho River, was a welcome setting in the beauty of the Texas heartland. (7) The Riveras explored the town's old Spanish buildings.

(8) Farther east, the urban landscape of Austin waited farther east. (9) The state capital is located along the Colorado River. (10) It offers a mix of technology, creativity, and live music. (11) Momma Rivera loves rock music. (12) The Riveras enjoyed their time in Austin. (13) They savored the scent of barbecue floating in the air as they strolled down Sixth Street.

(14) Houston, a busy big place, awaited to the southeast. (15) Skyscrapers appeared on the skyline. (16) These buildings prove the city's economic power in the energy and aerospace industries. (17) The Riveras marveled at the diversity that makes up Houston's culture.

(18) Next, the family explored the historical roots of Dallas and Fort Worth. (19) The cattle drives that shaped the Texas culture came to life right there, between modern skyscrapers and the historic stockyards. (20) The Riveras adored the blend of tradition and progress that defines these two cities.

(21) The road led south to the Gulf Coast. (22) The Riveras arrived at Galveston and Corpus Christi. (23) These cities are full of beach-going charm. (24) The Riveras enjoyed the Victorian buildings, tales of hurricanes, and coastal treasures along the sparkling waters of the Gulf of Mexico.

(25) The border town of El Paso marked the family's westernmost point. (26) El Paso is surrounded by mountains and is a gateway to the vast Chihuahuan Desert. (27) The city is located near many mountains. (28) Along the Rio Grande, the Riveras loved the unique blend of Texan and Mexican influences that shaped this southwestern town.

(29) The Riveras' road trip across Texas became more than a physical journey. (30) It became a story of exploration and connection. (31) They experienced the greatness of Texas culture and history.

PRACTICE #6 QUESTIONS

 Which sentence should replace sentence 2 to **BEST** state the central idea of this paper?

(1) The Riveras loved to take family road trips. **(2) They went somewhere together.** (3) The journey began in the sun-kissed deserts of West Texas, where Midland and Odessa stood on the horizon.

A) They all wondered where they should go first on the road trip they were taking.
B) They loved to travel together, and they did so whenever they could.
C) The family rented a van so everybody would have plenty of room.
D) Last summer, they set out on a road trip to the different cities of Texas.

 Which sentence would **BEST** follow and support sentence 7?

(7) The Riveras explored the town's old Spanish buildings.

A) The family wondered why they started off in San Angelo.
B) They loved exploring those old Spanish buildings.
C) They connected with the history of the city.
D) They couldn't wait to see Austin next.

 Sentence 8 repeats information. In the box provided, revise this sentence in a clear and effective way.

(8) Farther east, the urban landscape of Austin waited farther east.

_____
_____

 Lisa has included a sentence that does not belong in the third paragraph (sentences 8-13). Which sentence should she remove?

(8) Farther east, the urban landscape of Austin waited farther east. (9) The state capital is located along the Colorado River. (10) It offers a mix of technology, creativity, and live music. (11) Momma Rivera loves rock music. (12) The Riveras enjoyed their time in Austin. (13) They savored the scent of barbecue floating in the air as they strolled down Sixth Street.

A) Sentence 10
B) Sentence 11
C) Sentence 12
D) Sentence 13

 **#5** The meaning of sentence 14 is unclear. What word should replace **place** in this sentence?

(14) Houston, a busy, big place, awaited to the southeast.

A) location
B) building
C) city
D) direction

 #6 Which sentence would **BEST** follow and support sentence 17?

(17) The Riveras marveled at the diversity that makes up Houston's culture.

A) Their visit created lasting memories of Houston.
B) The Riveras enjoyed listening to podcasts while they traveled.
C) There are many tall buildings in Houston.
D) The traffic can be really heavy in big cities like Houston.

 #7 Lisa wants a more effective transition between the fourth paragraph (sentences 14-17) and the fifth paragraph (sentences 18-20). Select the **ONE** correct phrase that should replace **Next** in sentence 18 to improve this transition.

(18)
A) Crossing the prairies to the north,
B) When they were ready to go home,
C) While they were waiting at the gas station,
D) Although they were lost,

the family explored the historical roots of Dallas and Fort Worth.

 **#8** Which is the **BEST** way to combine sentences 21 and 22?

(21) The road led south to the Gulf Coast. (22) The Riveras arrived at Galveston and Corpus Christi.

A) Although the road led south to the Gulf Coast, the Riveras arrived at Galveston and Corpus Christi.
B) The road led south to the Gulf Coast, the Riveras arrived at Galveston and Corpus Christi.
C) As the road led south to the Gulf Coast, the Riveras arrived at Galveston and Corpus Christi.
D) Unless the road led south to the Gulf Coast, the Riveras arrived at Galveston and Corpus Christi.

 **#9** Read the seventh paragraph (sentences 25-28) again. Which sentence in this paragraph repeats information and should be removed?

(25) The border town of El Paso marked the family's westernmost point. (26) El Paso is surrounded by mountains and is a gateway to the vast Chihuahuan Desert. (27) The city is located near many mountains. (28) Along the Rio Grande, the Riveras loved the unique blend of Texan and Mexican influences that shaped this southwestern town.

A) Sentence 25
B) Sentence 26
C) Sentence 27
D) Sentence 28

 **#10** Which sentence would **BEST** follow and support sentence 31 to conclude this story?

(31) The Riveras experienced the greatness of Texas culture and history.

A) The family saved a lot of money by driving instead of flying, which helped them stay within their vacation budget.
B) Their adventure left them with lasting memories and a deeper appreciation for their home state.
C) Next summer, they hope to bring their dog along so the whole family can experience the fun together.
D) That's what the Riveras did on their road trip last summer.

REVISING: WARM-UP #7

Taylor wrote a short essay describing the Mountain Region of Texas. Read the essay and see what revisions she should make. Then answer the questions that follow.

Guide to the Mountains of West Texas

(1) This place is famous and unique. (2) It is located in the western part of the state. (3) The largest mountain range is the Guadalupe Mountains, home to the highest peak in Texas, Guadalupe Peak. (4) It stands at 8,751 feet above sea level. (5) This region also includes the Davis Mountains, Chisos Mountains, and Franklin Mountains, each adding to the unique topography of Texas.

(6) Guadalupe Mountains National Park is a place for fans of the outdoors. (7) The park offers hiking trails that wind through rugged canyons, leading to breathtaking things. (8) The Chihuahuan Desert extends into Texas' mountainous terrain. (9) This desert has dry landscapes and unique plants and animals that are adapted to the harsh desert environment.

(10) Plus, these mountains hold historical importance. (11) The Guadalupe Mountains were once part of an ancient underwater reef. (12) The remains of this geological past can be explored in the fossilized reefs found in the area. (13) Additionally, the region has played an important role in Native American and Western frontier history. (14) This is evident in the remains of native cultures and old mining sites.

(15) This region is home to many wildlife species living in different elevations and climates. (16) Mule deer, pronghorn, and a variety of bird species live in this ecosystem. (17) Visitors can experience many different natural wonders, from the beauty of desert landscapes to the cool pine forests at higher elevations. (18) Forests can be found up in the mountains.

(19) Texas' Mountains and Basins Region is a treasure of geological wonders, a treasure of rich history, and a treasure of vibrant ecosystems. (20) It invites explorers to marvel at the diverse landscapes that add to the Lone Star State's natural beauty.

REVISING: WARM-UP #7

#1 Which sentence should replace sentence 1 to **BEST** state the central idea of this paper?

(1) This place is famous and unique. (2) It is located in the western part of the state. (3) The largest mountain range is the Guadalupe Mountains, home to the highest peak in Texas, Guadalupe Peak.

A) I love going to the mountains!
B) The Mountains and Basins Region of Texas is known for its beautiful landscapes and diverse ecosystems.
C) Don't you want to know more about the mountains of Texas?
D) The Mountains and Basins Region of Texas is located in the western part of the state and has four mountain ranges.

#2 The meaning of sentence 7 is unclear. What word should replace **things** in this sentence?

(7) The park offers hiking trails that wind through rugged canyons, leading to breathtaking things.

A) trails
B) deserts
C) views
D) parks

#3 Taylor wants a more effective transition between the second paragraph (sentences 6-9) and the third paragraph (sentences 10-14). Select the **ONE** correct phrase that should replace **Plus** in sentence 10 to improve this transition.

(10)
A) In addition to their beauty,
B) Since they are historically important,
C) Because they are so lovely,
D) As they are being forgotten,

these mountains hold historical importance.

#4 Read the fourth paragraph (sentences 15-18) again. Which sentence in this paragraph repeats information and should be removed?

(15) This region is home to many wildlife species living in different elevations and climates. (16) Mule deer, pronghorn, and a variety of bird species live in this ecosystem. (17) Visitors can experience many different natural wonders, from the beauty of desert landscapes to the cool pine forests at higher elevations. (18) Forests can be found up in the mountains.

A) Sentence 15
B) Sentence 16
C) Sentence 17
D) Sentence 18

#5 Sentence 19 repeats information. In the box provided, revise this sentence in a clear and effective way.

(19) Texas' Mountains and Basins Region is a treasure of geological wonders, a treasure of rich history, and a treasure of vibrant ecosystems.

REVISING: PRACTICE #7

Lauren wrote a story about studying the regions of Texas. Read her story and see what revisions she should make. Then answer the questions that follow.

From Peaks to Prairies

(1) Sage, a fourth grader, loved adventure. (2) She started on a journey that went beyond the pages of her textbooks. (3) She did something special. (4) Sage's eyes sparkled with excitement as she began her exploration of the Mountains and Basins, Great Plains, North Central Plains, and Coastal Plains.

(5) With her maps, charts, and enthusiasm, Sage set out to identify the features of each region. (6) She used maps and charts. (7) The Mountains and Basins region, located in the westernmost part of Texas, fascinated her with its rough terrain and towering peaks. (8) Sage traced the outline of the Guadalupe Mountains. (9) She marveled at the desert landscapes and unique landforms.

(10) Next on her journey were the huge Great Plains. (11) They stretch across the northern part of the state. (12) Sage learned about the vast grasslands where buffalo once roamed freely. (13) Interested by tales of pioneers and cowboys, she pictured the sweeping prairies and the challenges faced by those who tamed this wild area. (14) Sage couldn't wait to get to the beach.

(15) The North Central Plains were Sage's next focus. (16) It's a region that has rolling hills. (17) It also has fertile soil. (18) She explored the Brazos River Valley and learned about the rich agricultural traditions of this part of Texas. (19) Sage admired the beautiful landscapes. (20) She studied the things of people who lived there once.

(21) She went somewhere different. (22) Here, she visited the Gulf of Mexico. (23) The Gulf's influence is evident in the warm climate and diverse vegetation. (24) The sight of marshes, the sight of beaches, and the sight of lush forests caught her eye.

(25) Sage didn't just stop at identification, but she also compared the regions. (26) She was amazed at how each area has its own climate, landforms, and vegetation. (27) Sage's understanding grew. (28) Then, she recognized the relationship between geography and the people who called each region home.

(29) Her geography project was mastered by Sage. (30) She also appreciated the wide variety of Texas's landscapes. (31) Her journey through Texas became proof of the importance of exploration and the joy of learning about the world.

PRACTICE #7 QUESTIONS

 **#1** Which sentence should replace sentence 3 to **BEST** state the central idea of this paper?

(1) Sage, a fourth grader, loved adventure. (2) She started on a journey that went beyond the pages of her textbooks. **(3) She did something special.** (4) Sage's eyes sparkled with excitement as she began her exploration of the Mountains and Basins, Great Plains, North Central Plains, and Coastal Plains.

A) She loved fourth grade and her social studies teacher.
B) She went on many different adventures.
C) She wanted to understand the different geographic regions of Texas.
D) Her favorite region is the Coastal Plains because of the beaches there.

 #2 Read the second paragraph (sentences 5-9) again. Which sentence in this paragraph repeats information and should be removed?

(5) With her maps, charts, and enthusiasm, Sage set out to identify the features of each region. (6) She used maps and charts. (7) The Mountains and Basins region, located in the westernmost part of Texas, fascinated her with its rough terrain and towering peaks. (8) Sage traced the outline of the Guadalupe Mountains. (9) She marveled at the desert landscapes and unique landforms.

A) Sentence 5
B) Sentence 6
C) Sentence 7
D) Sentence 8

 #3 Which is the **BEST** way to combine sentences 8 and 9?

(8) Sage traced the outline of the Guadalupe Mountains. (9) She marveled at the desert landscapes and unique landforms.

A) If Sage traced the outline of the Guadalupe Mountains, she marveled at the desert landscapes and unique landforms.
B) Sage traced the outline of the Guadalupe Mountains since she marveled at the desert landscapes and unique landforms.
C) As Sage traced the outline of the Guadalupe Mountains, she marveled at the desert landscapes and unique landforms.
D) Sage traced the outline of the Guadalupe Mountains, she marveled at the desert landscapes and unique landforms.

56 © Carlin Liborio

#4 Lauren has included a sentence that does not belong in the third paragraph (sentences 10-14). Which sentence should she remove?

(10) Next on her journey were the huge Great Plains. (11) They stretch across the northern part of the state. (12) Sage learned about the vast grasslands, where buffalo once roamed freely. (13) Interested by tales of pioneers and cowboys, she pictured the sweeping prairies and the challenges faced by those who tamed this wild area. (14) Sage couldn't wait to get to the beach.

A) Sentence 11
B) Sentence 12
C) Sentence 13
D) Sentence 14

#5 Which is the **BEST** way to combine sentences 16 and 17?

(16) It's a region that has rolling hills. (17) It also has fertile soil.

A) It's a region that has rolling hills if it also has fertile soil.
B) When it's a region that has rolling hills, it also has fertile soil.
C) It's a region that has rolling hills and fertile soil.
D) It's a region that has rolling hills until it also has fertile soil.

#6 The meaning of sentence 20 is unclear. What word should replace **things** in this sentence?

(19) Sage admired the beautiful landscapes. (20) She studied the things of people who lived there once.

A) hills
B) objects
C) communities
D) directions

#7 Lauren needs a better topic sentence for the fifth paragraph (sentences 21-24). Which sentence should replace sentence 21?

(21) She went somewhere different. (22) Here, she visited the Gulf of Mexico. (23) The Gulf's influence is evident in the warm climate and diverse vegetation. (24) The sight of marshes, the sight of beaches, and the sight of lush forests caught her eye.

A) Sage moved on to a different region.
B) Next she visited the Gulf of Mexico.
C) There's much more to know about the regions of Texas.
D) Sage's adventure took her to the eastern shores of Texas.

© Carlin Liborio

#8 Sentence 24 repeats information. In the box provided, revise this sentence in a clear and effective way.

(24) The sight of marshes, the sight of beaches, and the sight of lush forests caught her eye.

#9 Lauren wants a more effective transition between sentence 27 and sentence 28 in the sixth paragraph (sentences 25-28). Select the **ONE** correct phrase that should replace **Then** in sentence 28 to improve this transition.

(28)
A) At the same time,
B) Even though,
C) On the other hand,
D) In conclusion,

she recognized the relationship between geography and the people who called each region home.

#10 Sentence 29 needs to be revised. In the box provided, revise this sentence in a clear and effective way.

(29) Her geography project was mastered by Sage.

58

© Carlin Liborio

Part 2: Editing

Editing Strategies Checklist

Warm-Up #1: American Indian Origins
Practice #1A: American Indian Groups & #1B: Exploring Texas

Warm-Up #2: Finding Out About Energy
Practice #2A: Electric Circle &
#2B: Wagon Force

Warm-Up #3: Catholic Missions in Texas
Practice #3A: The Father of Texas & #3B: Fight for Freedom

Warm-Up #4: Backyard Investigations
Practice #4A: Backyard Bird Feeder &
#4B: Park Lesson

Warm-Up #5: Sink or Float?
Practice #5A: Examining Soils & #5B: Weathering

Warm-Up #6: The Texas Revolution
Practice #6A: James Bowie & #6B: Juan Antonio Padilla

Warm-Up #7: Renewable Resources
Practice #7A: Nonrenewable Resources &
#7B: Conservation

Editing Strategies:

- ☑ Highlight the key words in the question.
- ☑ Highlight the sentence or paragraph in the passage.
- ☑ Read the sentence/paragraph out loud (or use a whisper phone).
- ☑ Try each answer choice.
- ☑ Eliminate/cross out answers that do not make sense.
- ☑ Choose the answer that makes the most sense.
- ☑ Lastly, justify your answer!

Revise	Edit
ARMS	CUPS
A Add sentences and words.	**C** Capitals: sentences, names, places, months, titles, I
R Remove words or sentences.	**U** Usage: match nouns and verbs correctly, grammar usage
M Move a word or sentence.	**P** Punctuation: . ! ? ' , " "
S Substitute words or sentences.	**S** Spelling: Check all words, use your resources.

What is EDITING?

- Editing is the process of ensuring the **correctness** of your writing. Is it **correct** or not?

- Editing is **c**apitalization, **u**sage of grammar, **p**unctuation, and **s**pelling!

- Editing is **reviewing** and **fixing** your conventions so that people can understand it!

EDITING: WARM-UP #1

Lara is writing a paper for her social studies class. Read these paragraphs from the beginning of Lara's paper and look for corrections she needs to make. Then answer the questions that follow.

American Indian Origins

(1) The origins of American Indian groups in Texas trace back thousands of years. (2) Early people likely migrated from Asia across a land bridge called Beringia during the ice age. (3) These early migrants spread across North and South America, and some eventually settled in the region we now know as Texas.

(4) Over time, different groups developed their own cultures and way's of life. (5) They adapted to Texas's diverse environments, such as deserts, plains, forests, and coastlines. (6) Some groups, such as the Caddo in East Texas, built permanent villages and were skilled farmers. (7) They growed crops like corn, beans, and squash. (8) Others, like the Comanche in the plains, were nomadic and hunted buffalo.

(9) These American Indian groups lived in Texas long before European explorers arrived. (10) The exact details of their migration are still debated by archaeologists. (11) Its clear that the ancestors of these groups were among the first to call Texas home. (12) There rich cultures and traditions left a lasting impact on the history of Texas.

 What change should be made in sentence 2?

(2) Early people likely migrated from Asia across a land bridge called Beringia during the ice age.

A) Change **likely** to **like**
B) Change **bridge** to **bridges**
C) Change **during** to **toward**
D) Change **ice age** to **Ice Age**

#2 Lara has written sentence 4 incorrectly. Select the response that corrects this sentence.

(4) Over time, different groups developed their own cultures and

A) weigh
B) ways
C) way
D) weigh's

of life.

#3 What change should be made in sentence 7?

(7) They growed crops like corn, beans, and squash.

A) Change **They** to **Them**
B) Change **growed** to **grew**
C) Change **corn, beans, and squash** to **Corn, Beans, and Squash**
D) Remove the comma after **corn**

#4 What change should be made in sentence 11?

(11) Its clear that the ancestors of these groups were among the first to call Texas home.

A) Change **Its** to **It's**
B) Change **these** to **this**
C) Change **groups** to **Groups**
D) Change **were** to **was**

#5 What change should be made in sentence 12?

(12) There rich cultures and traditions left a lasting impact on the history of Texas.

A) Change **There** to **Their**
B) Change **traditions** to **tradition's**
C) Change **left** to **lefted**
D) Change **Texas** to **texas**

EDITING: PRACTICE #1A

Wendy is writing a paper for her social studies class. Read these paragraphs from the beginning of Wendy's paper and look for corrections she needs to make. Then answer the questions that follow.

American Indian Groups

(1) Before European explorers came to Texas, the land was home to several American Indian groups, each with their own culture and traditions. (2) Their differences was based on where they were located and the resources around them. (3) In East Texas, the Caddo people were skilled farmers. (4) They built permanent homes out of wood and grass and grew crops like corn, beans, and squash. (5) The Caddo lived in villages and had a strong system of government leaded by chiefs.

(6) On the other hand, the Comanche and Apache lived in the planes of Central and West Texas. (7) They didn't stay in one place but moved around to follow the buffalo herds. (8) Buffalo were very important to them because they was providing food, clothing, and materials for shelter. (9) Comanche and Apache lived in tipis, which were easy to take down and set up as they traveled.

(10) Near the Gulf Coast, the Karankawa people lived a different life. (11) They were hunters and gatherers. (12) They fished, hunted small animals, and gathered food like berries and nuts. (13) They moved with the seasons but stayed near the coast to use it's resources.

#1 What change should be made in sentence 2?

(2) Their differences was based on where they were located and the resources around them.

A) Change **differences** to **difference**
B) Change **was** to **were**
C) Change **where** to **when**
D) Insert a comma after **located**

#2 What change should be made in sentence 5?

(5) The Caddo lived in villages and had a strong system of government leaded by chiefs.

A) Change **Caddo** to **caddo**
B) Change **lived** to **are living**
C) Change **villages** to **vilages**
D) Change **leaded** to **led**

#3 What change should be made in sentence 6?

(6) On the other hand, the Comanche and Apache lived in the planes of Central and West Texas.

A) Change **Comanche and Apache** to **comanche and apache**
B) Change **lived** to **was living**
C) Change **in** to **under**
D) Change **planes** to **plains**

#4 Wendy has written sentence 8 incorrectly. Select the response that corrects this sentence.

(8) Buffalo were very important to them because they food, clothing, and materials for shelter.

A) provided
B) are providing
C) provide
D) was provided

#5 What change should be made in sentence 13?

(13) They moved with the seasons but stayed near the coast to use it's resources.

A) Change **seasons** to **season's**
B) Insert a comma after **seasons**
C) Change **use** to **used**
D) Change **it's** to **its**

EDITING: PRACTICE #1B

Fatima is writing a paper for her social studies class. Read these paragraphs from the beginning of Fatima's paper and look for corrections she needs to make. Then answer the questions that follow.

Exploring Texas

(1) European explorers came to Texas for a few reasons. (2) First, they were searching for wealth. (3) Many Europeans believed that Texas had gold or other valuable resources. (4) Spanish explorers have hoped to find riches like those discovered in other regions of the New World.

(5) Another reason was the desire for land. European countries like Spain and France wanted to expand their empires. (6) Texas was seen as a new place to claim and settel. (7) By exploring and establishing colonies, they could increase their power and influence.

(8) Religion also played a big role. (9) Spanish explorers wanted to spread Christianity to the native peoples of Texas. (10) They built missions and communities where they teached American Indians about their religion and way of life.

(11) Finally, some explorers came for adventure. (12) The idea of discovering new lands, meeting new people, and exploring unknown territorys excited many Europeans. (13) They wanted to make a name for them and bring glory to their home countries.

#1 Fatima has written sentence 4 incorrectly. Select the response that corrects this sentence.

(4) Spanish explorers [A) were hoping / B) are hoping / C) will hope / D) was hoping] to find riches like those discovered in other regions of the New World.

 **What change should be made in sentence 6?**

(6) Texas was seen as a new place to claim and settel.

A) Change **seen** to **saw**
B) Change **new** to **knew**
C) Insert a comma after **claim**
D) Change **settel** to **settle**

 What change should be made in sentence 10?

(10) They built missions and communities where they teached American Indians about their religion and way of life.

A) Change **built** to **builded**
B) Change **communities** to **communitys**
C) Change **teached** to **taught**
D) Change **their** to **there**

 **What change should be made in sentence 12?**

(12) The idea of discovering new lands, meeting new people, and exploring unknown territorys excited many Europeans.

A) Change **meeting** to **met**
B) Change **territorys** to **territories**
C) Change **many** to **mini**
D) Change **Europeans** to **europeans**

 Fatima has written sentence 13 incorrectly. Select the response that corrects this sentence.

(13) They wanted to make a name for ⟨⟩ and bring glory to their home countries.

A) themselves
B) theirselfs
C) themself
D) himself

EDITING: WARM-UP #2

Veronica is writing a paper for her science class. Read these paragraphs from the beginning of Veronica's paper and look for corrections she needs to make. Then answer the questions that follow.

Finding Out About Energy

(1) Ryan and Kelly were best friends in fourth grade and they both loved learning new things. (2) One day, their teacher introduced the topic of energy in science class.

(3) "There are many types of energy around us," she explained.

(4) Ryan and Kelly were excited to find out more.

(5) First, they learned about mechanical energy. (6) When Kelly kicked a soccer ball, it rolled across the field. (7) That was mechanical energy, the energy of movement. (8) Then they hear the school bell ring. (9) Their teacher explained that it was sound energy traveling through the air to their ears.

(10) They discovered electrical energy when Ryan fliped the light switch in the classroom. (11) The lights turned on because electrical energy flowed through the wires. (12) Kelly pointed out the sunlight coming with the window.

(13) That's light energy, she said proudly. (14) "Light energy helps us see and can even warm us up!"

 What change should be made in sentence 1?

(1) Ryan and Kelly were best friends in fourth grade and they both loved learning new things.

A) Change **were** to **was**
B) Change **friends** to **friend's**
C) Insert a comma after **grade**
D) Change **both** to **all**

#2 Select the response that corrects the error in sentence 8.

(8) Then they [A) heard / B) are hearing / C) heared / D) will hear] the school bell ring.

#3 What change should be made in sentence 10?

(10) They discovered electrical energy when Ryan fliped the light switch in the classroom.

A) Change **discovered** to **discover**
B) Change **energy** to **energys**
C) Change **fliped** to **flipped**
D) Change **in** to **on**

#4 Veronica has written sentence 12 incorrectly. Select the response that corrects this sentence.

(12) Kelly pointed out the sunlight coming [A) to / B) for / C) around / D) through] the window.

#5 Select the response that corrects the error in sentence 13.

(13) That's light energy, she said proudly.

A) "That's light energy, she said proudly."
B) "That's light energy," she said proudly.
C) "That's light energy, she said" proudly.
D) That's light energy, "she said proudly."

EDITING: PRACTICE #2A

Aaliyah is writing a paper for her science class. Read these paragraphs from the beginning of Aaliyah's paper and look for corrections she needs to make. Then answer the questions that follow.

Electric Circle

(1) Nikki and Sal loved fourth-grade science. (2) On lab day, their teacher showed them a lightbulb, a battery, and some wires. (3) "We're going to learn how electricity works," she said. (4) Nikki and Sal was excited to figure it out.

(5) First, they connected the wires to the battery, but nothing happened. (6) "Why won't the lightbulb turn on" Sal asked.

(7) Their teacher explained, "Electricity needs a closed path, or circuit, to flow."

(8) Nikki think for a moment and then said, "Let's try making a complete loop." (9) They attached one wire from the battery to the lightbulb. (10) Then they used another wire to conect the lightbulb back to the battery. (11) Suddenly, the lightbulb turned on! (12) Both kids cheered.

(13) Nikki and Sal were thrilled. (14) They realized that for electricity to work, it needs to travel in a circle, just like a racetrack! (15) They couldn't wait to build more circuits explore how other electrical devices worked.

#1 Aaliyah has written sentence 4 incorrectly. Select the response that corrects this sentence.

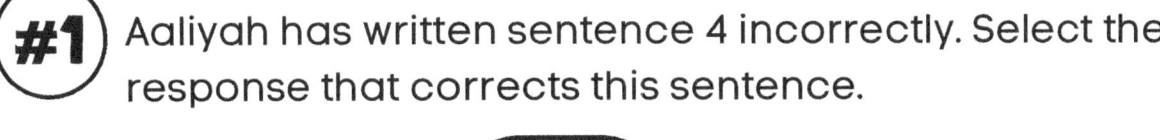

(4) Nikki and Sal [A) are / B) were / C) is / D) wasn't] excited to figure it out.

#2 What change should be made in sentence 6?

(6) "Why won't the lightbulb turn on" Sal asked.

A) Remove the quotation marks after **on**
B) Change **won't** to **not**
C) Insert a question mark after **on**
D) Replace the period with a question mark

#3 What change should be made in sentence 8?

(8) Nikki think for a moment and then said, "Let's try making a complete loop."

A) Change **think** to **thought**
B) Insert a comma after **moment**
C) Change **Let's** to **Lets**
D) Change **making** to **made**

#4 What change should be made in sentence 10?

(10) Then they used another wire to conect the lightbulb back to the battery.

A) Change **they** to **them**
B) Change **another** to **Another**
C) Change **conect** to **connect**
D) Change **to** to **too**

#5 What is the correct way to write sentence 15?

(15) They couldn't wait to build more circuits explore how other electrical devices worked.

A) They couldn't wait to build more circuits. Explore how other electrical devices worked.
B) They couldn't wait to build more circuits, explore how other electrical devices worked.
C) They couldn't wait to build more circuits explore. How other electrical devices worked.
D) They couldn't wait to build more circuits and explore how other electrical devices worked.

EDITING: PRACTICE #2B

Sabrina is writing a paper for her science class. Read these paragraphs from the beginning of Sabrina's paper and look for corrections she needs to make. Then answer the questions that follow.

Wagon Force

(1) Rico and Dimitri were playing with a toy wagon in the park. (2) Rico decided to pull the wagon with a rope. (3) The wagon started moving for him.

(4) "Look, Dimitri," Rico said, "I'm using force to move the wagon!"

(5) Dimitri was curious, so he gave the wagon a push from the other side. (6) The wagon moved faster rolled away from them.

(7) "That was cool!" said Dimitri. (8) "When I push the wagon, it moves the same way I push it!"

(9) Then Rico had an idea.

(10) "What happens if we both push it from opposite sides?"

(11) They each pushed, the wagon didn't move.

(12) "That's because our forces are canceling each other out!" Rico exclaimed.

(13) Dimitri realized that if the forces are equal and in opposite directions, the object doesn't move.

(14) They experimented with more pushes and pulls. (15) Rico and Dimitri learned that forces can make object move, stop, or even stay still. (16) It all depends on how hard and in which direction the force is applyed. (17) It was a fun leson on the power of force!

#1 Sabrina has written sentence 3 incorrectly. Select the response that corrects this sentence.

(3) The wagon started moving _____ him.

A) in
B) within
C) toward
D) between

#2 Select the response that corrects the error in sentence 6.

(6) The wagon moved faster rolled away from them.

A) The wagon moved faster and rolled away from them.
B) The wagon moved faster, rolled away, from them.
C) The wagon moved faster. Rolled away from them.
D) The wagon moved faster, the wagon rolled away from them.

#3 What change should be made in sentence 11?

(11) They each pushed, the wagon didn't move.

A) They each pushed unless the wagon didn't move.
B) They each pushed the wagon didn't move.
C) They each pushed, but the wagon didn't move.
D) They each pushed then the wagon didn't move.

#4 What change should be made in sentence 16?

(16) It all depends on how hard and in which direction the force is applyed.

A) Change **It** to **Its**
B) Change **hard** to **heard**
C) Change **applyed** to **applied**
D) Replace the period with a question mark

#5 What change should be made in sentence 17?

(17) It was a fun leson on the power of force!

A) Change **was** to **were**
B) Change **fun** to **funner**
C) Change **leson** to **lesson**
D) Change **force** to **Force**

EDITING: WARM-UP #3

Brenda is writing a paper for her social studies class. Read these paragraphs from the beginning of Brenda's paper and look for corrections she needs to make. Then answer the questions that follow.

Catholic Missions in Texas

(1) In the late 1600s, Spain wanted to expand it's control over new lands, including the area we now call Texas. (2) They were especially interested in the area of Texas because other countries, like France, were also exploring and claiming land nearby.
(3) Spain worryed that if they didn't settle the land, other countries would. (4) They decided to build settlements and missions to claim the land.

(5) The missions were usually builded near rivers, like the San Antonio River. (6) Water was important for farming and everyday life. (7) Some missions were set up in places that are now cities, like San Antonio and El Paso. (8) The goals were to spread Christianity and to teach the Native American people new ways of farming, and living. (9) Spanish priests were known as friars they worked hard to teach Native Americans about the Catholic faith.

 What change should be made in sentence 1?

(1) In the late 1600s, Spain wanted to expand it's control over new lands, including the area we now call Texas.

A) Change **wanted** to **wants**
B) Change **it's** to **its**
C) Change **over** to **under**
D) Change **lands** to **land's**

 **#2** Brenda has written sentence 3 incorrectly. Select the response that corrects this sentence.

(3) Spain
- A) worried
- B) was worryed
- C) worry
- D) worrying

that if they didn't settle the land, other countries would.

 **#3** What change should be made in sentence 5?

(5) The missions were usually builded near rivers, like the San Antonio River.

A) Change **missions** to **mission**
B) Change **were** to **was**
C) Change **builded** to **built**
D) Change **rivers** to **Rivers**

 #4 What change should be made in sentence 8?

(8) The goals were to spread Christianity and to teach the Native American people new ways of farming, and living.

A) Change **were** to **was**
B) Change **teach** to **taught**
C) Change **new** to **knew**
D) Remove the comma after **farming**

 #5 Select the response that corrects the error in sentence 9.

(9) Spanish priests were known as friars they worked hard to teach Native Americans about the Catholic faith.

A) Spanish priests were known as friars and they worked hard. To teach Native Americans about the Catholic faith.
B) Spanish priests were known as friars, they worked hard to teach Native Americans about the Catholic faith.
C) Spanish priests were known as friars, but they worked hard to teach Native Americans about the Catholic faith
D) Spanish priests were known as friars, and they worked hard to teach Native Americans about the Catholic faith.

© **Carlin Liborio**

EDITING: PRACTICE #3A

Coco is writing a paper for her social studies class. Read these paragraphs from the beginning of Coco's paper and look for corrections she needs to make. Then answer the questions that follow.

The Father of Texas

(1) Stephen F. Austin is known as the "Father of Texas." (2) In the early 1820s, Austin led settlers from the United States to settle in Texas, which was then part of Mexico. (3) His bigger accomplishment was founding the first major colony of Americans in Texas. (4) The original group of 300 settlers were known as the "Old Three Hundred." (5) Austin worked hard to follow mexican laws and keep peace between the settlers and the government. (6) As a result, he was able to bring in more people, and the colony grew larger.

(7) Austin was motivated by economic reasons too. (8) He believed Texas had great land for farming, and he knew that more settlers would make the area grow and become wealthy. (9) Each new family that joined his colony bringed money, trade, and new skills. (10) Austin hoped that these settlers would create economic activity.

(11) Austin's work didn't just make Texas richer. (12) It also led to more settlements and a stronger community. (13) His efforts set the stage for Texas to gain independence, this made him an important figure in Texas history.

#1 Coco has written sentence 3 incorrectly. Select the response that corrects this sentence.

(3) His
A) biggest
B) more big
C) most biggest
D) most big
accomplishment was founding the first major colony of Americans in Texas.

What change should be made in sentence 5?

(5) Austin worked hard to follow mexican laws and keep peace between the settlers and the government.

A) Change **worked** to **work**
B) Change **follow** to **folow**
C) Change **mexican** to **Mexican**
D) Change **settlers** to **settler's**

What change should be made in sentence 9?

(9) Each new family that joined his colony bringed money, trade, and new skills.

A) Change **family** to **families**
B) Change **colony** to **Colony**
C) Change **bringed** to **brought**
D) Change **new** to **knew**

What change should be made in sentence 12?

(12) It also led to more settelments and a stronger community.

A) Change **led** to **leaded**
B) Change **settelments** to **settlements**
C) Change **stronger** to **more stronger**
D) Change **community** to **communities**

What change should be made in sentence 13?

(13) His efforts set the stage for Texas to gain independence, this made him an important figure in Texas history.

A) His efforts set the stage for Texas to gain independence until this made him an important figure in Texas history.
B) His efforts set the stage for Texas to gain independence this made him an important figure in Texas history.
C) Although his efforts set the stage for Texas to gain independence, this made him an important figure in Texas history.
D) His efforts set the stage for Texas to gain independence, and this made him an important figure in Texas history.

EDITING: PRACTICE #3B

Red is writing a paper for her social studies class. Read these paragraphs from the beginning of Red's paper and look for corrections she needs to make. Then answer the questions that follow.

Fight for Freedom

(1) Texas played an important role in the Mexican War of Independence. (2) At the time, Texas was part of Mexico and was controled by Spain. (3) People in Mexico wanted freedom from Spanish rule, and some Texans joined the fight for independence. (4) In some battles, Texan and Mexican rebels worked together to push out Spanish forces. (5) The Battle of Medina was unsuccessful, it inspired others to keep fighting for freedom.

(6) Mexico finally won independence in 1821 Texas became a part of the new country of Mexico. (7) This changed Texas in big ways. (8) The new Mexican government encouraged settlers from the United States to move to Texas to help grow the population and strengthen the region. (9) This is when Stephen F. Austin brought settlers to Texas. (10) They started the first American colonys. (11) However, the differences between American settlers and the Mexican government eventually led to conflicts.

(12) The mexican war of independence helped shape Texas.

 What change should be made in sentence 2?

(2) At the time, Texas was part of Mexico and controled by Spain.

A) Change **was** to **is**
B) Insert a comma after **Mexico**
C) Change **controled** to **controlled**
D) Change **Spain** to **spain**

#2 Select the response that corrects the error in sentence 5.

(5) The Battle of Medina was unsuccessful, it inspired others to keep fighting for freedom.

A) Although the Battle of Medina was unsuccessful, it inspired others to keep fighting for freedom.
B) The Battle of Medina was unsuccessful. It inspired others. To keep fighting for freedom.
C) The Battle of Medina was unsuccessful next it inspired others to keep fighting for freedom.
D) Unless this battle was unsuccessful, it inspired others to keep fighting for freedom.

#3 Select the response that corrects the error in sentence 6.

(6) Mexico finally won independence in 1821 Texas became a part of the new country of Mexico.

A) Mexico finally won independence in 1821 then Texas became a part of the new country of Mexico.
B) Mexico finally won independence in 1821 Texas became. A part of the new country of Mexico.
C) Mexico finally won independence in 1821, Texas became a part of the new country of Mexico.
D) When Mexico finally won independence in 1821, Texas became a part of the new country of Mexico.

#4 What change should be made in sentence 10?

(10) They started the first American colonys.

A) Change **They** to **They're**
B) Change **started** to **start**
C) Change **colonys** to **colonies**
D) Change the period to a question mark

#5 Red has written sentence 12 incorrectly. Select the response that corrects this sentence.

(12) The _____ helped shape Texas.

A) Mexican war of independence
B) Mexican War of Independence
C) Mexican war of Independence
D) Mexican War of independence

EDITING: WARM-UP #4

Tamara is writing a paper for her science class. Read these paragraphs from the body of Tamara's paper and look for corrections she needs to make. Then answer the questions that follow.

Backyard Investigations

(1) Luke and Lily's first mission was to examine the plants. (2) They noticed that some leaves were smooth and shiny, while others were rough and bumpy.

(3) Next, they looked around for insects and spotted an ant trail. (4) The ants were carrying crumbs and tiny bits of leaves back to their colony. (5) Luke gentle scooped an ant into the jar so they could look at it more closely with the magnifying glass.

(6) "They're so tiny but so strong!" Luke observed."

(7) "They must be collecting food to bring back to the others," Lily added.

(8) They heared a buzzing sound. (9) It was a bee moving from flower to flower! (10) Luke and Lily remembered learning that bees help plants grow by spreading pollen. (11) They watched the bee for a while they decided to write all their discoveries in a report. (12) Their investigation in their own backyard had taught them so much about the amazing world of plants and insects!

 What change should be made in sentence 3?

(3) Next, they looked around for insects and spoted an ant trail.

A) Change **looked** to **looks**
B) Change **for** to **from**
C) Change **spoted** to **spotted**
D) Change **ant** to **aunt**

#2 Tamara has written sentence 5 incorrectly. Select the response that corrects this sentence.

(5) Luke [A) gently B) more gentle C) gentler D) most gentle] scooped an ant into the jar so they could look at it more closely with the magnifying glass.

#3 Select the response that corrects the error in sentence 6.

(6) "They're so tiny but so strong!" Luke observed."

A) They're so tiny but so strong! Luke observed.
B) They're so tiny but so strong! "Luke observed."
C) "They're so tiny but so strong! Luke observed."
D) "They're so tiny but so strong!" Luke observed.

#4 Tamara has written sentence 8 incorrectly. Select the response that corrects this sentence.

(8) They [A) hearing B) heard C) hear D) hears] a buzzing sound.

#5 Select the response that corrects the error in sentence 11.

(11) They watched the bee for a while they decided to write all their discoveries in a report

A) They watched the bee for a while, they decided to write all their discoveries in a report.
B) They watched the bee for a while before they decided to write all their discoveries in a report.
C) They watched the bee for a while. And decided to write all their discoveries in a report.
D) They watched the bee for a while. Deciding to write all their discoveries in a report.

80 © Carlin Liborio

EDITING: PRACTICE #4A

Katie is writing a paper for her science class. Read these paragraphs from the beginning of Katie's paper and look for corrections she needs to make. Then answer the questions that follow.

Backyard Bird Feeder

(1) Rachel and David were excited to set up a bird feeder in their backyard. (2) They wanted to attract different types of birds they had a problem. (3) They didn't know which seeds would work best! (4) They knew they had to use critical thinking and problem-solving skills to make the right choice.

(5) First, they made a list of all the seed types they could try—sunflower seeds, millet, and peanuts. (6) Then, Rachel and David did some research. (7) They discovered that different seeds attract different types of birds.

(8) "We should try to attract as many birds as we can, David suggested."

(9) Next, they created a plan. (10) They decided to fill three different feeders: one with sunflower seeds, one with millet, and one with peanuts. (11) They would observe each feeder every day for a week and record the types of birds they saw.

(12) At the end of the week, they reviewed their notes. (13) The sunflower seed feeder attracted the most birds. (14) Decided that would be their main choice. (15) They also choosed to add a little millet and peanuts to keep the smaller birds happy. (16) Rachel and David had used their research, careful planning, and observations to make a smart decision. (17) Their backyard quick became a bird paradise!

#1 Select the response that corrects the error in sentence 2.

(2) They wanted to attract different types of birds they had a problem.

A) They wanted to attract different types of birds, but they had a problem.
B) They wanted to attract different types of birds, they had a problem.
C) They wanted to attract different types of birds. Had a problem.
D) They wanted to attract. Different types of birds. They had a problem.

 **#2** Select the response that corrects the error in sentence 8.

(8) "We should try to attract as many birds as we can, David suggested."

A) "We should try to attract as many birds as we can, David suggested.
B) "We should try to attract as many birds as we can," David suggested."
C) We should try to attract as many birds as we can, "David suggested."
D) "We should try to attract as many birds as we can," David suggested.

 **#3** What is the correct way to write sentences 13 and 14?

(13) The sunflower seed feeder attracted the most birds.
(14) Decided that would be their main choice.

A) The sunflower seed feeder attracted the most birds, decided that would be their main choice.
B) The sunflower seed feeder attracted the most birds, so they decided that would be their main choice.
C) The sunflower seed feeder attracted the most birds. And decided that would be their main choice.
D) The sunflower seed feeder attracted the most birds. Deciding that would be their main choice.

 **#4** Katie has written sentence 15 incorrectly. Select the response that corrects this sentence.

(15) They also
A) choosing
B) chosen
C) chose
D) had choosed
to add a little millet and peanuts to keep the smaller birds happy.

 **#5** Katie has written sentence 17 incorrectly. Select the response that corrects this sentence.

(17) Their backyard
A) quicker
B) more quicker
C) quickest
D) quickly
became a bird paradise!

EDITING: PRACTICE #4B

Mei is writing a paper for her science class. Read these paragraphs from the beginning of Mei's paper and look for corrections she needs to make. Then answer the questions that follow.

Park Lesson

(1) Mackenzie and Blanca went for a walk in the park. (2) They noticed all kinds of plants around them. (3) Animals too. (4) As they walked, Mackenzie spotted a small tree with yellowing leaves.

(5) "I wonder why this tree looks" sick, she said.

(6) Blanca thought about it and replied, "Maybe it's not getting enough water or sunlight. (7) Plants need those to grow!"

(8) Just then, they saw a family of squirrels digging in the ground. (9) Looking for nuts. (10) "Why are they berrying food?" Mackenzie asked.

(11) Blanca remembered something she had learned in school and explained, "Animals, just like plants, have basic needs." (12) Squirrels hide food for later so they can eat during winter when there's less food around." (13) Mackenzie nodded. (14) She realized that food, water, and shelter was all needed for animals to survive.

 What is the correct way to write sentences 2 and 3?

(2) They noticed all kinds of plants around them. (3) Animals too.

A) They noticed all kinds of plants around them, so animals too.
B) They noticed all kinds of plants and animals around them.
C) They noticed all kinds of plants around them. Some animals too.
D) They noticed all kinds of plants. Around them with animals too.

 Select the response that corrects the error in sentence 5.

(5) "I wonder why this tree looks" sick, she said.

A) "I wonder why this tree looks sick," she said.
B) "I wonder why this tree looks sick, she said."
C) I wonder why this tree looks sick, she said.
D) I wonder why this tree looks sick, "she said."

 Select the response that corrects the error.

(8) Just then, they saw a family of squirrels digging in the ground. (9) Looking for nuts.

A) Just then, they saw a family of squirrels digging in the ground. And looking for nuts.
B) Just then, they saw a family of squirrels. They were digging in the ground and looking for nuts.
C) Just then, they saw a family of squirrels. Digging in the ground and looking for nuts.
D) Just then, they saw a family of squirrels. Digging in the ground. Looking for nuts.

 What change should be made in sentence 10?

(10) "Why are they berrying food?" Mackenzie asked.

A) Remove the quotation marks before **Why**
B) Change **are** to **is**
C) Change **berrying** to **burying**
D) Remove the period after **asked**

#5 What change should be made in sentence 14?

(14) She realized that food, water, and shelter was all needed for animals to survive.

A) Change **realized** to **realizes**
B) Remove the comma **food**
C) Change **was** to **were**
D) Change **animals** to **animal's**

EDITING: WARM-UP #5

Hahn is writing a paper for her science class. Read these paragraphs from the beginning of Hahn's paper and look for corrections she needs to make. Then answer the questions that follow.

Sink or Float?

(1) Max, Molly, and Kendra were excited about today's science experiment. (2) Their teacher had set up a big tub of water their mission was to discover which objects could sink or float. (3) They each brought a few items from home.

(4) Max dropped a rock into the water. (5) Watched it settle at the bottom of the tub. (6) "It's because rocks are heavy," Max guessed.

(7) Molly wanted to try next. (8) She picked up a leaf and placed it gently on the waters surface. (9) "Look! The leaf is floating!" she cheered. (10) The leaf bobbed gently, barely making a splash. (11) "I think it floats because it's so light," Molly explained." (12) Kendra had another idea.

(13) "Maybe it's not just about weight," Kendra said. (14) She picked up the rubber ball and dropped it in. (15) It floated too, even though it was more heavy than the leaf. (16) "See, some heavy things can float if they're filled with air," she said.

 Hahn made an error in sentence 2. Which response corrects the error?

(2) Their teacher had set up a big tub of water their mission was to discover which objects could sink or float.

A) Their teacher had set up a big tub of water, and their mission was to discover which objects could sink or float.
B) Their teacher had set up a big tub of water. And their mission was to discover which objects could sink or float.
C) Their teacher had set up. A big tub of water. Their mission was to discover which objects could sink or float.
D) Their teacher had set up a big tub of water, their mission was to discover. Which objects could sink or float.

 **What is the correct way to write sentences 4 and 5?**

(4) Max dropped a rock into the water. (5) Watched it settle at the bottom of the tub.

A) Max watching it settle at the bottom of the tub.
B) Max dropped a rock into the water and watched it settle at the bottom of the tub.
C) Max dropped a rock into the water then he watched it settle at the bottom of the tub.
D) Max dropped a rock. Into the water and watched it settle at the bottom of the tub.

 **What change should be made in sentence 8?**

(8) She picked up a leaf and placed it gently on the waters surface.

A) Change **picked** to **picks**
B) Change **placed** to **placing**
C) Change **gently** to **gentle**
D) Change **waters** to **water's**

 **What change should be made in sentence 11?**

(11) "I think it floats because it's so light," Molly explained."

A) Change **think** to **thinks**
B) Change **because** to **cause**
C) Change **it's** to **its**
D) Remove the quotation marks after **explained**

 What change should be made in sentence 15?

(15) It floated too, even though it was more heavy than the leaf.

A) Change **it** to **it's**
B) Change **too** to **two**
C) Change **more heavy** to **heavier**
D) Change **than** to **then**

EDITING: PRACTICE #5A

Hannah is writing a paper for her science class. Read these paragraphs from the beginning of Hannah's paper and look for corrections she needs to make. Then answer the questions that follow.

Examining Soils

(1) Daisy and Nora were excited for the day's science lesson about soil. (2) Their teacher gived each of them a set of soil samples from different places.

(3) They looked at the color of each soil. (4) The sandy soil was light tan. (5) The garden soil was dark brown, the clay was a reddish-brown. (6) "I wonder if the color tells us anything about what plants might grow best in each one," Daisy said thoughtful.

(7) Then, they tested each soils ability to hold water. (8) They poured the same amount of water onto each type and watched. (9) The water drained through the sand quickly but stayed mostly on top of the clay. (10) The garden soil drained some water but didn't got too wet.

#1 Hannah made an error in sentence 2. Which response corrects the error?

(2) Their teacher
A) gave
B) has gived
C) was given
D) giving
 each of them a set of soil samples from different places.

#2 Select the response that corrects the error in sentence 5.

(5) The garden soil was dark brown, the clay was a reddish-brown.

A) The garden soil was dark brown the clay was a reddish-brown.
B) The garden soil was dark brown the clay. Was a reddish-brown.
C) The garden soil was dark brown, and the clay was a reddish-brown.
D) The garden soil was dark brown, so the clay was a reddish-brown.

#3 What change should be made in sentence 6?

(6) "I wonder if the color tells us anything about what plants might grow best in each one," Daisy said thoughtful.

A) Change **tells** to **tell**
B) Change **about** to **around**
C) Change **best** to **most best**
D) Change **thoughtful** to **thoughtfully**

#4 What change should be made in sentence 7?

(7) Then, they tested each soils ability to hold water.

A) Change **Then** to **Than**
B) Change **tested** to **tests**
C) Change **ability** to **abilitys**
D) Change **soils** to **soil's**

#5 What change should be made in sentence 10?

(10) The garden soil drained some water but didn't got too wet.

A) Change **drained** to **drain**
B) Insert a comma after **water**
C) Change **got** to **get**
D) Change **too** to **to**

EDITING: PRACTICE #5B

Kenzie is writing a paper for her science class. Read these paragraphs from the beginning of Kenzie's paper and look for corrections she needs to make. Then answer the questions that follow.

Weathering

(1) Kendrick and Patrick were on a hike with their science class. (2) They were exploring nature. (3) Learning about Earth's surface. (4) Their teacher explained that the ground beneath their feet was always changing. (5) Sometimes it would change in ways too slow to notice. (6) He called this process "weathering."

(7) Mr. Lee pointed out a large rock with cracks and small peaces breaking off. (8) "Look closely, boys," he said. (9) "This rock is breaking down. (10) That's weathering." (11) Kendrick noticed the rough edges of the rock. (12) Wind, rain, and even tiny bits of sand weared it down over time.

(13) Patrick spotted a tree root pushing up through a sidewalk nearby. (14) "Whoa! (15) It looks as if the root is breaking the ground!" he exclaimed. (16) Mr. Lee explained that tree roots can cause weathering too. (17) As they grow, they push against rocks and soil. (18) This causes cracks and breaks things apart slow.

#1 What is the correct way to write sentences 2 and 3?

(2) They were exploring nature. (3) Learning about Earth's surface.

A) They were exploring nature and learning about Earth's surface.
B) They were exploring nature, they were learning about Earth's surface.
C) They were exploring nature, but learning about Earth's surface.
D) They were exploring nature. And learning about Earth's surface.

 What change should be made in sentence 7?

(7) Mr. Lee pointed out a large rock with cracks and small peaces breaking off.

A) Change **rock** to **Rock**
B) Change **cracks** to **crack's**
C) Change **peaces** to **pieces**
D) Change **breaking** to **broke**

 Kenzie made an error in sentence 12. Which response corrects the error?

(12) Wind, rain, and even tiny bits of sand ⬚ it down over time.

A) wear
B) has weared
C) had worn
D) wearing

 What change should be made in sentence 13?

(13) Patrick spotted a tree root pushing up through a sidewalk nearby.

A) Change **spoted** to **spotted**
B) Change **tree** to **trees**
C) Change **pushing** to **were pushing**
D) Change **sidewalk** to **sidewalk's**

#5 Kenzie made an error in sentence 18. Which response corrects the error?

(18) This causes cracks and breaks things apart ⬚

A) most slowest.
B) more slower.
C) slowing.
D) slowly.

EDITING: WARM-UP #6

Holly is writing a paper for her social studies class. Read these paragraphs from the beginning of Holly's paper and look for corrections she needs to make. Then answer the questions that follow.

The Texas Revolution

(1) The Texas Revolution was a big fight between Texas and Mexico in 1835-1836. (2) It started because Texas settlers didn't like the Mexican governments rules. (3) They wanted more freedom to make their own decisions. (4) The conflict quickly turned into a war for independence.

(5) One of the first major events was the Battel of Gonzales in October 1835. (6) Mexican soldiers came to take back a cannon from the Texans, but the Texans refused. (7) They even put up a flag that said, "Come and Take It!" (8) This small fight started the revolution.

(9) Another important event was the Siege of the Alamo in February 1836. (10) The Mexican army surrounded the Alamo. (11) About 200 Texans defending it. (12) The Mexican troops defeated the Texans, and almost all the defenders were killed. (13) Even though the Texans lost, "Remember the Alamo!" became a rallying cry for their cause.

(14) Shortly after, Texas leaders declared independence from Mexico on March 2, 1836. (15) Then came the Battle of San Jacinto in April. (16) The last big battle. (17) The Texas army was led by General Sam Houston. (18) They surprised and defeated Santa Anna's troops in just 18 minutes. (19) This victory winned Texas independence.

 What change should be made in sentence 2?

(2) It started because Texas settlers didn't like the Mexican governments rules.

A) Change **settlers** to **settler**
B) Change **didn't** to **doesn't**
C) Change **Mexican** to **mexican**
D) Change **governments** to **government's**

#2 What change should be made in sentence 5?

(5) One of the first major events was the Battel of Gonzales in October 1835.

A) Change **One** to **Won**
B) Change **major** to **Major**
C) Change **Battel** to **Battle**
D) Change **Gonzalez** to **gonzalez**

#3 Holly made an error in sentence 11. Which response corrects the error?

(11) About 200 Texans defending it.

A) About 200 Texans defended it.
B) And about 200 Texans defended it.
C) With about 200 Texans defending it.
D) There was about 200 Texans defending it.

#4 What is the correct way to write sentences 15 and 16?

(15) Then came the Battle of San Jacinto in April. (16) The last big battle.

A) Then came the Battle of San Jacinto in April it was the last big battle.
B) Then came the Battle of San Jacinto in April. It was the last big battle.
C) Then came the Battle of San Jacinto. In April, the last big battle.
D) Then came the Battle of San Jacinto in April. And was the last big battle.

#5 Holly made an error in sentence 19. Which response corrects the error?

(19) This victory
A) wins
B) winning
C) won
D) wonned
Texas independence.

EDITING: PRACTICE #6A

Daniella is writing a paper for her social studies class. Read these paragraphs from the beginning of Daniella's paper and look for corrections she needs to make. Then answer the questions that follow.

James Bowie

(1) James Bowie was an important leader during the Texas Revolution. (2) Born in Kentucky in 1796, Bowie became famous for his bravery and strength. (3) One of his biggest contributions to history were the invention of the Bowie knife. (4) This is a large blade used for survival and fighting.

(5) In Texas, Bowie joined the settlers who wanted freedom from Mexican rule. (6) Bowie was a very dedicated man. (7) He was known for being fearless and he stood up for what he believed was right. (8) Bowie became a key leader in the fight for Texas independence. (9) He was trusted by others for his determination and his skill in battle.

(10) One of his most famous moments came at the Battle of the Alamo. (11) Bowie helped defend the Alamo against a much large Mexican army. (12) Even though Bowie was very sick during the battle, he continued to give orders and inspire the troops. (13) The defenders of the Alamo lost the battle their courage motivated others to join the fight for Texas independence.

(14) James Bowie is remembered as a hero who gave his life to help Texas gain it's freedom. (15) His bravery at the Alamo became a symbol of standing strong even in the face of overwhelming challenges.

 What change should be made in sentence 3?

(3) One of his biggest contributions to history were the invention of the Bowie knife.

A) Change **biggest** to **most big**
B) Change **history** to **historys**
C) Change **were** to **was**
D) Change the period to a question mark

What change should be made in sentence 7?

(7) He was known for being fearless and he stood up for what he believed was right.

A) Change **was** to **were**
B) Insert a comma after **fearless**
C) Change **believed** to **beleived**
D) Change **right** to **write**

What change should be made in sentence 11?

(11) Bowie helped defend the Alamo against a much large Mexican army.

A) Change **helped** to **helps**
B) Change **defend** to **defending**
C) Change **Alamo** to **alamo**
D) Change **large** to **larger**

Select the response that corrects the error in sentence 13.

(13) The defenders of the Alamo lost the battle their courage motivated others to join the fight for Texas independence.

A) The defenders of the Alamo lost the battle, their courage motivated others to join the fight for Texas independence.
B) The defenders of the Alamo lost the battle, but their courage motivated others to join the fight for Texas independence.
C) The defenders of the Alamo lost the battle their courage. Motivated others to join the fight for Texas independence.
D) The defenders of the Alamo lost. The battle their courage motivated others to join the fight for Texas independence.

What change should be made in sentence 14?

(14) James Bowie is remembered as a hero who gave his life to help Texas gain it's freedom.

A) Change **remembered** to **remembering**
B) Change **gave** to **gived**
C) Change **life** to **lives**
D) Change **it's** to **its**

EDITING: PRACTICE #6B

Luis is writing a paper for his social studies class. Read these paragraphs from the beginning of Luis' paper and look for corrections he needs to make. Then answer the questions that follow.

Juan Antonio Padilla

(1) Juan Antonio Padilla played an important roll during the time of the Texas Revolution. (2) He was a Mexican official and lawyer who believed in fairness and justice. (3) Padilla worked as an official in Texas when it was still part of Mexico. (4) His work helped organize land grants for settlers this brought many people to Texas.

(5) Padilla became a supporter of the Texians when they wanted independence from Mexico. (6) He believed that the government in Mexico City was not treating Texans fairly. (7) Wanted to see changes. (8) Padilla used his knowledge of law and government to help the settlers understand their rights and how to organize for independence.

(9) Padilla did not fight in battles but he helped in other important ways. (10) He supported the settlers' ideas of creating a new government and stood up for their cause. (11) Padilla also helped build strong relationships between different groups in Texas to unite them during the revolution.

(12) Padilla's contributions remind us that fighting for freedom isn't just about battles. (13) It's also about ideas, fairness, and bringing people together. (14) His efforts helped Texas grow more stronger while it worked to become an independent republic.

#1 What change should be made in sentence 1?

(1) Juan Antonio Padilla played an important roll during the time of the Texas Revolution.

A) Change **played** to **playing**
B) Change **roll** to **role**
C) Change **time** to **Time**
D) Change **Revolution** to **revolution**

#2 Select the response that corrects the error in sentence 4.

(4) His work helped organize land grants for settlers this brought many people to Texas.

A) His work helped organize land grants. For settlers this brought many people to Texas.
B) His work helped organize land grants for settlers, this brought many people to Texas.
C) His work helped organize land grants for settlers. This brought. Many people to Texas.
D) His work helped organize land grants for settlers, which brought many people to Texas.

#3 What is the correct way to write sentences 6 and 7?

(6) He believed that the government in Mexico City was not treating Texans fairly. (7) Wanted to see changes.

A) He believed that the government in Mexico City was not treating Texans fairly, wanted to see changes.
B) He believed that the government in Mexico City was not treating Texans fairly and wanted to see changes.
C) He believed that the government in Mexico City was not treating Texans fairly. Wanting to see changes.
D) He believed that the government in Mexico City was not treating Texans fairly and wanted to see them. The changes.

#4 What change should be made in sentence 9?

(9) Padilla did not fight in battles but he helped in other important ways.

A) Change **did** to **was**
B) Change **battles** to **battle's**
C) Insert a comma after **battles**
D) Change **helped** to **helps**

#5 Luis made an error in sentence 14. Which response corrects the error?

(14) His efforts helped Texas grow [A) stronger B) most strong C) strongest D) was strong] while it worked to become an independent republic.

EDITING: WARM-UP #7

Brenda is writing a paper for her science class. Read these paragraphs from the beginning of Brenda's paper and look for corrections she needs to make. Then answer the questions that follow.

Renewable Resources

(1) Blanca and Bella were two best friends who loved exploring nature. (2) They desided to learn about Earth's renewable resources. (3) These are things nature provides that can be used over and over again if we take care of them.

(4) First, they stood in a meadow, feeling the breeze on their faces. (5) "Air is a renewable resource," Blanca said." (6) "We can't see it, but it's always around us."

(7) They reached a forest and Bella pointed to the towering trees. (8) "Plants, like these trees, are renewable because they grow back. (9) We use them for food, shelter, and even air!"

(10) Blanca and Bella realized that renewable resources are amazeing gifts from nature. (11) "But we have to use them wisely," said Blanca. (12) "If we waste or pollute them, they might not last."

(13) The friends promised to care for these resources. (14) They knowed their small actions could make a big difference for the planet.

#1 What change should be made in sentence 2?

(2) They desided to learn about Earth's renewable resources.

A) Change **desided** to **decided**
B) Change **learn** to **learning**
C) Change **about** to **around**
D) Change **Earth's** to **Earths**

 Brenda made an error in sentence 5. Which response corrects the error?

(5) "Air is a renewable resource," Blanca said."

A) "Air is a renewable resource, Blanca said."
B) "Air is a renewable resource," Blanca said.
C) Air is a renewable resource, "Blanca said."
D) "Air is a renewable resource, Blanca" said.

 What change should be made in sentence 7?

(7) They reached a forest and Bella pointed to the towering trees.

A) Change **reached** to **reaches**
B) Change **forest** to **Forest**
C) Insert a comma after **forest**
D) Change **pointed** to **points**

 What change should be made in sentence 10?

(10) Blanca and Bella realized that renewable resources are amazeing gifts from nature.

A) Change **realized** to **realizes**
B) Change **are** to **is**
C) Change **amazeing** to **amazing**
D) Change **from** to **under**

 Select the response that corrects the error in sentence 14.

(14) They
A) known
B) knowing
C) knows
D) knew
their small actions could make a big difference for the planet.

98
© Carlin Liborio

EDITING: PRACTICE #7A

Lilliana is writing a paper for her science class. Read these paragraphs from the beginning of Lilliana's paper and look for corrections she needs to make. Then answer the questions that follow.

Nonrenewable Resources

(1) Rose and Julia were curious fourth graders who enjoyed solving nature's mysteries. (2) One day, their teacher challenged them to learn about Earth's nonrenewable resources. (3) These are things we use from nature and can't be replaced once there gone.

(4) They started near an old mineing site. (5) "This is coal," Rose said, holding a small black rock. (6) "People burn it to make electricity but it takes millions of years to form. (7) Once we use it all, it's gone!"

(8) Next, they visited an oil rig by the sea. (9) Julia pointed to the machines pumping dark liquid from deep underground. (10) "That's oil," she explained. (11) "It powers cars and planes. (12) Just like coal, it cant be made quickly."

(13) Their last stop was a natural gas plant a worker showed them how invisible gas is piped from the Earth. (14) "Natural gas is cleaner than coal and oil," Rose said, "but it's still nonrenewable."

#1 What change should be made in sentence 3?

   (3) These are things we use from nature and can't be replaced once there gone.

A) Change **are** to **is**
B) Change **use** to **uses**
C) Change **can't** to **cant**
D) Change **there** to **they're**

#2 What change should be made in sentence 4?

(4) They started near an old mineing site.

A) Change **started** to **starts**
B) Change **near** to **into**
C) Change **mineing** to **mining**
D) Change **site** to **sight**

#3 What change should be made in sentence 6?

(6) People burn it to make electricity but it takes millions of years to form.

A) Change **make** to **making**
B) Insert a comma after **electricity**
C) Change **takes** to **take**
D) Change **years** to **year's**

#4 What change should be made in sentence 12?

(11) "It powers cars and planes. (12) **Just like coal, it cant be made quickly.**"

A) Change **coal** to **cole**
B) Change **cant** to **can't**
C) Change **made** to **make**
D) Change **quickly."** to **quickly.**

#5 Select the response that corrects the error in sentence 13.

(13) Their last stop was a natural gas plant a worker showed them how invisible gas is piped from the Earth.

A) Their last stop was a natural gas plant. A worker showed them how invisible gas is piped from the Earth.
B) Their last stop was a natural gas. Plant a worker showed them how invisible gas is piped from the Earth.
C) Their last stop was a natural gas plant, a worker showed them how invisible gas is piped from the Earth.
D) Their last stop was a natural gas plant, and showed them how invisible gas is piped from the Earth.

EDITING: PRACTICE #7B

Zara is writing a paper for her science class. Read these paragraphs from the beginning of Zara's paper and look for corrections she needs to make. Then answer the questions that follow.

Conservation

(1) Ms. Rivera was a fourth-grade teacher. (2) One day, she brought a big box to class. (3) "Today, we're talking about conservation. (4) Conservation is about protecting our planet's resources. (5) Let's see whats in the box!" she said.

(6) Ms. Rivera showed a small potted plant. (7) "Plants are renewable resources but they need care. (8) If we cut down too many trees or pollute the soil, they won't grow back as quickly. (9) Planting trees and gardens helps!"

(10) Then, she holded up a water jug. (11) "Water is essential for life, but clean water isn't endless. (12) Turning off faucets and fixing leaks helps conserve it."

(13) Finally, she pulled out a picture of the sun. (14) The students learned that solar energy is renewable. (15) Doesn't run out. (16) Using the sun, wind, or water for power instead of coal or oil helps keep Earth clean.

(17) Ms. Rivera smiled at her students. (18) "Conservation is about making smart choices, like recycling, saving water, planting trees, and useing renewable energy. (19) Even small actions, like turning off lights, can make a big difference."

 What change should be made in sentence 5?

(3) "Today, we're talking about conservation. (4) Conservation is about protecting our planet's resources. **(5) Let's see whats in the box!" she said.**

A) Change **see** to **sea**
B) Change **whats** to **what's**
C) Remove the quotation marks after **box!**
D) Insert quotation marks after **said**.

#2 What change should be made in sentence 7?

(6) Ms. Rivera showed a small potted plant. **(7) "Plants are renewable resources but they need care.** (8) If we cut down too many trees or pollute the soil, they won't grow back as quickly. (9) Planting trees and gardens helps!"

A) Delete the quotation marks before **Plants**
B) Change **are** to **is**
C) Insert a comma after **resources**
D) Change **care** to **careful**

#3 Select the response that corrects the error in sentence 10.

(10) Then, she ___ up a water jug.

A) held
B) holds
C) holding
D) hold

#4 What is the correct way to write sentences 14 and 15?

(14) The students learned that solar energy is renewable.
(15) Doesn't run out.

A) The students learned that solar energy is renewable. And doesn't run out.
B) The students learned that solar energy is renewable, it doesn't run out.
C) The students learned that solar energy. Is renewable. Doesn't run out.
D) The students learned that solar energy is renewable, so it doesn't run out.

#5 What change should be made in sentence 18?

(17) Ms. Rivera smiled at her students. **(18) "Conservation is about making smart choices, like recycling, saving water, planting trees, and useing renewable energy.** (19) Even small actions, like turning off lights, can make a big difference."

A) Remove the quotation marks before **Conservation**
B) Remove the comma after **water**
C) Change **useing** to **using**
D) Change **energy** to **energys**

Revise 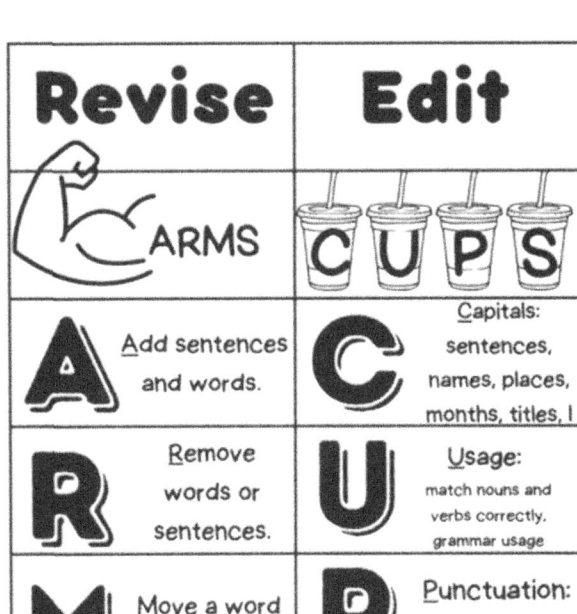 ARMS	Edit CUPS
Add sentences and words.	**C**apitals: sentences, names, places, months, titles, I
Remove words or sentences.	**U**sage: match nouns and verbs correctly, grammar usage
Move a word or sentence.	**P**unctuation: . ! ? ' , " "
Substitute words or sentences.	**S**pelling: Check all words, use your resources.

© Carlin Liborio

104

© Carlin Liborio

REVISING ANSWER KEYS

WARM-UP #1

1.	C
2.	C
3.	D
4.	D
5.	**Possible Answer**: It makes our lives more interesting and full of possibilities.

WARM-UP #2

1.	A
2.	**Possible Answer**: It connected people across great distances and changed the ways we communicate.
3.	D
4.	B
5.	**Possible Answer**: It allows for instant messaging, social media, and access to information.

WARM-UP #3

1.	A
2.	C
3.	**Possible Answer**: It is more than just a work of art.
4.	C
5.	D

WARM-UP #4

1.	B
2.	**A**
3.	D
4.	B
5.	**C**

WARM-UP #5

1.	D
2.	**Possible Answer**: The storm quickly got stronger.
3.	A
4.	C
5.	D

WARM-UP #6

1.	D
2.	**Possible Answer**: The city's diverse population created a unique culture.
3.	A
4.	D
5.	D

WARM-UP #7

1.	B
2.	C
3.	A
4.	D
5.	**Possible Answer**: Texas' Mountains and Basins Region is a treasure of geological wonders, rich history, and vibrant ecosystems.

PRACTICE #1

1.	B	6.	A
2.	B	7.	D
3.	D	8.	B
4.	C	9.	C
5.	A	10.	**Possible Answer**: Ashley's gardening and plant business showed how the free enterprise system worked.

PRACTICE #2

1.	D	6.	B
2.	**Possible Answer**: He was home earlier in the evenings, so the family had more time to spend together.	7.	C
3.	D	8.	A
4.	**Possible Answer**: It allowed them to look up exciting new games and chat with friends from far-off places.	9.	C
5.	A	10.	**Possible Answer**: In many ways, the lives of people like Izzy, Daniel, and Carlos improved.

REVISING ANSWER KEYS

PRACTICE #3

1.	C	6.	B
2.	D	7.	C
3.	B	8.	**Possible Answer**: Each flag and landmark had a story of hardship, victory, and the fight for freedom.
4.	C	9.	C
5.	**Possible Answer**: They left a lasting mark on Texas history.	10.	A

PRACTICE #4

1.	D	6.	**Possible Answer**: She learned how electrical energy powers many devices in everyday life and about the importance of conductors and insulators.
2.	**Possible Answer**: To begin with, mechanical energy sparked Claudia's curiosity.	7.	D
3.	A	8.	B
4.	D	9.	C
5.	C	10.	D

PRACTICE #5

1.	C	6.	D
2.	**Possible Answers**: As the thunder roared and lightning flashed, the old cowboy took shelter in a cave. **OR** The old cowboy took shelter in a cave as the thunder roared and lightning flashed.	7.	B
3.	A	8.	**Possible Answer**: The townsfolk were amazed by his skill(s).
4.	D	9.	A
5.	C	10.	D

PRACTICE #6

1.	D	6.	A
2.	C	7.	A
3.	**Possible Answer**: The urban landscape of Austin waited farther east.	8.	C
4.	B	9.	C
5.	C	10.	B

PRACTICE #7

1.	C	6.	C
2.	B	7.	D
3.	C	8.	**Possible Answer**: The sight of marshes, beaches, and lush forests caught her eye.
4.	D	9.	A
5.	C	10.	**Possible Answer**: Sage mastered her geography project.

EDITING ANSWER KEYS

WARM-UP #1

1.	D
2.	B
3.	B
4.	A
5.	A

PRACTICE #1A

1.	B
2.	D
3.	D
4.	A
5.	D

PRACTICE #1B

1.	A
2.	D
3.	C
4.	B
5.	A

WARM-UP #2

1.	C
2.	A
3.	C
4.	D
5.	B

PRACTICE #2A

1.	B
2.	C
3.	A
4.	C
5.	D

PRACTICE #2B

1.	C
2.	A
3.	C
4.	C
5.	C

WARM-UP #3

1.	B
2.	A
3.	C
4.	D
5.	D

PRACTICE #3A

1.	A
2.	C
3.	C
4.	B
5.	D

PRACTICE #3B

1.	C
2.	A
3.	D
4.	C
5.	B

WARM-UP #4

1.	C
2.	A
3.	D
4.	B
5.	B

PRACTICE #4A

1.	A
2.	D
3.	B
4.	C
5.	D

PRACTICE #4B

1.	B
2.	A
3.	B
4.	C
5.	C

© Carlin Liborio

EDITING ANSWER KEYS

WARM-UP #5

1.	A
2.	B
3.	D
4.	D
5.	C

PRACTICE #5A

1.	A
2.	C
3.	D
4.	D
5.	C

PRACTICE #5B

1.	A
2.	C
3.	C
4.	A
5.	D

WARM-UP #6

1.	D
2.	C
3.	A
4.	B
5.	C

PRACTICE #6A

1.	C
2.	B
3.	D
4.	B
5.	D

PRACTICE #6B

1.	B
2.	D
3.	B
4.	C
5.	A

WARM-UP #7

1.	A
2.	B
3.	C
4.	C
5.	D

PRACTICE #7A

1.	D
2.	C
3.	B
4.	B
5.	A

PRACTICE #7B

1.	B
2.	C
3.	A
4.	D
5.	C

© Carlin Liborio

Made in the USA
Coppell, TX
11 February 2026